I0455842

Editor-in-Chief and Founder:
Lyndon H. LaRouche, Jr.
Editorial Board: *Lyndon H. LaRouche, Jr. , Helga
Zepp-LaRouche, Robert Ingraham, Tony
Papert, Gerald Rose, Dennis Small, Jeffrey
Steinberg, William Wertz*
Co-Editors: *Robert Ingraham, Tony Papert*
Managing Editor: *Nancy Spannaus*
Technology: *Marsha Freeman*
Books: *Katherine Notley*
Ebooks: *Richard Burden*
Graphics: *Alan Yue*
Photos: *Stuart Lewis*
Circulation Manager: *Stanley Ezrol*

INTELLIGENCE DIRECTORS
Counterintelligence: *Jeffrey Steinberg, Michele
Steinberg*
Economics: *John Hoefle, Marcia Merry Baker,
Paul Gallagher*
History: *Anton Chaitkin*
Ibero-America: *Dennis Small*
Russia and Eastern Europe: *Rachel Douglas*
United States: *Debra Freeman*

INTERNATIONAL BUREAUS
Bogotá: *Miriam Redondo*
Berlin: *Rainer Apel*
Copenhagen: *Tom Gillesberg*
Houston: *Harley Schlanger*
Lima: *Sara Madueño*
Melbourne: *Robert Barwick*
Mexico City: *Gerardo Castilleja Chávez*
New Delhi: *Ramtanu Maitra*
Paris: *Christine Bierre*
Stockholm: *Ulf Sandmark*
United Nations, N.Y.C.: *Leni Rubinstein*
Washington, D.C.: *William Jones*
Wiesbaden: *Göran Haglund*

ON THE WEB
e-mail: eirns@larouchepub.com
www.larouchepub.com
www.executiveintelligencereview.com
www.larouchepub.com/eiw
Webmaster: *John Sigerson*
Assistant Webmaster: *George Hollis*
Editor, Arabic-language edition: *Hussein Askary*

EIR (ISSN 0273-6314) *is published weekly
(50 issues), by EIR News Service, Inc.,
P.O. Box 17390, Washington, D.C. 20041-0390.
(703) 777-9451*

European Headquarters: E.I.R. GmbH, Postfach
Bahnstrasse 9a, D-65205, Wiesbaden, Germany
Tel: 49-611-73650
Homepage: http://www.eirna.com
e-mail: eirna@eirna.com
Director: Georg Neudecker

Montreal, Canada: 514-461-1557

Denmark: EIR - Danmark, Sankt Knuds Vej 11,
basement left, DK-1903 Frederiksberg, Denmark.
Tel.: +45 35 43 60 40, Fax: +45 35 43 87 57. e-mail:
eirdk@hotmail.com.

Mexico City: EIR, Sor Juana Inés de la Cruz 242-2
Col. Agricultura C.P. 11360
Delegación M. Hidalgo, México D.F.
Tel. (5525) 5318-2301
eirmexico@gmail.com

Canada Post Publication Sales Agreement
#40683579

Postmaster: Send all address changes to *EIR*, P.O.
Box 17390, Washington, D.C. 20041-0390.

Signed articles in *EIR* represent the views of the
authors, and not necessarily those of the Editorial
Board.

Deutsche Bank Must Be Saved for the Sake of World Peace

EDITORIAL

Deutsche Bank Must Be Saved, for the Sake of World Peace!

Statement issued by Helga Zepp-LaRouche, Chairwoman of the German Civil Rights Movement Solidarity (BüSo), on July 12, 2016.

The imminent threat of the bankruptcy of Deutsche Bank is certainly not the only potential trigger for a new systemic crisis of the trans-Atlantic banking system, which would be orders of magnitude more deadly than the 2008 crisis, but it does offer a unique lever to prevent a collapse into chaos.

Behind the SOS launched by the chief economist of Deutsche Bank, David Folkerts-Landau, for an EU program of €150 billion to recapitalize the banks, lurks the danger openly discussed in international financial media, that the entire European banking system is de facto insolvent, and is sitting on a mountain of at least €2 trillion of non-performing loans. Deutsche Bank is the international bank which, with a total of €55 trillions of outstanding derivative contracts and a leverage factor of 40:1, even outdoes Lehman Brothers at the time of its collapse, and therefore represents the most dangerous Achilles heel of the system. Half of Deutsche Bank's balance sheet, which has plummeted 48% in the past 12 months and is down to only 8% of its peak value, is made up of level-3 derivatives, i.e., derivatives amounting to circa €800 billion without a market valuation.

It probably came as a surprise to many that Lyndon LaRouche called today for Deutsche Bank to be saved through a one-time increase in its capital base, because of the systemic implications of its threatened bankruptcy. Neither the German government with its GDP of €4 trillion, nor the EU with a GDP of €18 trillion, would be able to control the domino effect of a disorderly bankruptcy.

The one-time capital injection, LaRouche explained, is only an emergency measure which needs to be followed by an immediate reorientation of the bank, back to its tradition which prevailed until 1989 under the leadership of Alfred Herrhausen. To actually oversee such an operation, a management committee must be set up to verify the legitimacy and the implications of the obligations, and finalize its work within a given timeframe. That committee should also draw up a new business plan, based on Herrhausen's banking philosophy and exclusively oriented to the interests of the real economy of Germany.

Alfred Herrhausen was the last actually creative, moral industrial banker of Germany. He defended, among other things, the cancellation of the unpayable debt of developing countries, as well as the long-term credit financing of well-defined development projects. In December 1989, he planned to present in New York a plan for the industrialization of Poland, which was consistent with the criteria used by the *Kreditanstalt für Wiederaufbau* (KfW) for the post-1945 reconstruction of Germany, and would have offered a completely different perspective than the so-called "reform policy," or shock therapy, of Jeffrey Sachs.

Herrhausen was assassinated on November 30, 1989 by the "Third Generation of the Red Army Fraction," whose existence has yet to be proven to this day. It happened only two days after Chancellor Helmut Kohl, who counted Herrhausen among his closest advisors, had presented his ten-point program for gradually overcoming the division of Germany [between East and West]. The *cui bono* of the terrorist attack remains one of the most fateful issues in the modern history of Germany, and one which urgently needs to be clarified.

The fact is that Herrhausen's successors introduced a fundamental paradigm change in the bank's philosophy, which brought Deutsche Bank into the wild world of profit maximization at all costs, and also into countless unpunishable and punishable legal entanglements, which those responsible have avoided until now, mainly because of the "too big to fail" premises.

The transformation of Deutsche Bank into a global investment bank with the highest derivatives exposure, combined with the simultaneous credit crunch for German small and medium-sized enterprises, is symptomatic of the folly which has led to the current catastrophe.

We must now act with resolution, but not in the way Folkerts-Landau proposes, that is, not with more of the same medicine, which would certainly kill the patient.

Although it has mainly operated over the past years out of London and New York, Deutsche Bank is too important for the German economy, and therefore for Germany, and ultimately for the fate of all of Europe. Its reorganization in the spirit of Alfred Herrhausen is not only the key to overcoming the banking crisis, but also for averting the acute danger of war.

Herrhausen's assassination has gone unpunished. However, there exists "the dreaded might, that judges what is hid from sight," which is the subject of Friedrich Schiller's poem "Die Kraniche des Ibykus." The Erinyes have begun their dreadful dance.[1]

It is now incumbent upon all those who, in addition to the family, have suffered from the assassination of Herrhausen, upon the representatives of the Mittelstand, of the German economy, and the institutional representatives of the German population, to honor his legacy and to seize the tremendous opportunity which is now offered to save Germany.

---

1. Friedrich Schiller, "Die Kraniche des Ibykus."

EIR Contents

www.larouchepub.com Volume 43, Number 29, July 15, 2016

Cover This Week

Alfred Herrhausen, 1930-1989

I. Leibniz

FOR THE LEIBNIZ YEAR 2016

Do You Know Gottfried Wilhelm Leibniz?

by Martin Kaiser

The origin of the most central, fundamental, and most memorable of those deeper roots of my presently knowledgeable outlook, is to be located in my reaction to a study, dating from my adolescence, on the subject of Gottfried Leibniz's concept of the Monadology.[1]

—Lyndon LaRouche

This is an edited translation of "Kennen Sie Gottfried Wilhelm Leibniz? Zum Leibnizjahr 2016," which appeared in Germany in Neue Solidarität, *March 2, 2016.*

March 2—This year's 300th anniversary of the death of Gottfried Wilhelm Leibniz provokes the question: What could be the reason for the change from the phases of growth and flourishing of societies, to their downfall? Although today's common sense assumes that societies come and go like seasons, Leibniz was not of this conviction. Growing up in the rubble of what was left of cities, villages, farms, and fields by the Thirty Years' War (1618-1648), where more than 30 percent of the European

Gottfried Wilhelm Leibniz, 1646-1716, in a portrait by Christoph Bernard Francke, about 1700.

population was eliminated, he was not of today's liberal disposition, that fate decides where societies go and that one cannot do anything about it.

Since the trend of our society is set against its own survival, with possibly both a global financial crash and a world war bringing it to a sudden end, it is worthwhile to delve intensively into the life of Leibniz, if we want to escape from our fatal course. For Leibniz inspired so many contemporaries and successors to end the remnants of feudalism, initiate another Renaissance, and found a new form of society, that he can be considered, without exaggeration, the source of our idea of a moral state.

Why, for example, did a collapse of European civilization follow after the Italian Renaissance in the 15th Century? Wasn't it the hallmark of the Renaissance to view man as the crown of God's creation, so that science flourished as well as economic and artistic activity? Didn't poverty and ignorance recede, when the human being was seen as the living image of the highest creative principle? The citizens' participation in the state even awakened memories of the ancient Athenian democracy.

1. *EIR*, Feb. 22, 2008.

But no single achievement of this golden hour of mankind, between the Middle Ages and the religious wars in the 16th and 17th centuries with their barbarism, can adequately explain the principle of the Renaissance itself. Inspired by the Platonic idea of human reason, man again began to discover new laws of nature, art, and mind, in order to make them accessible to all mankind. Nicolas of Cusa and Leonardo da Vinci are still known for their pioneering roles, which have served mankind down to today.

The relationship between man and the Cosmos was revolutionized, and human beings no longer saw themselves—through their superstitions—as victims of blind forces of nature, but rather as agents of the creative principle.

Leibniz Challenges the Oligarchy

In Gottfried Wilhelm Leibniz (1646-1716), the oligarchical masters of Europe encountered an adversary who brought the ideas of the Renaissance to new heights, unlocked new powers of nature for mankind like a Prometheus, and thus ensured its survival. He intervened in all social spheres to develop his vision of a general harmony, a *Harmonia Universalis*. No sharper opposition can be conceived than that between Leibniz and his contemporary Thomas Hobbes (1588-1679), who created for the British Empire then arising in the footsteps of Rome, the ideology by which "every man is a wolf to every other."

In contrast to this, Leibniz saw in the creative potentials of every human being—his or her inventive spirit in skilled crafts, science, the arts, or mining—the mainspring of the good state, and thereby became the founder of the science of economics. In his early work, *Society and Science* (1671), the 25-year-old Leibniz drafted a program which we today would perhaps regard as contemporary, and which later led to his efforts to found scientific academies. He wrote:

Monopoly is avoided, since this society always wants to pay [only] the fair price,— or even more cheaply in many cases, by causing manufactured goods to be produced locally [rather than imported]. It will especially preclude the formation of a monopoly of merchants ... along with excessive accumulation of wealth by the merchants or excessive poverty of the artisans— which is particularly the case in Holland, where the merchants are riding high, whereas the artisans are kept in continual poverty and toil ... And why, indeed, should so many people be poor and miserable for the benefit of such a small handful? After all, is not the entire purpose of society to release the artisan from his misery?... The society's highest rule shall be to foster true love and tolerance among its members, and not to express anything irritating, scornful, or insulting to others.[2]

For Leibniz, this was consonant with the best ordering of Creation, and that for him was the reason, based in natural law, that the state should strive for this end. For according to the arbitrary will of the absolutist rulers, the result of government was in one case collapse and misery, in another progress, as it served the growth of their power and ambition. But they hardly saw themselves as in service of a universal development. Leibniz' principle was "to work for the public welfare, without being concerned whether anyone thanks me for it." As the grounds for it, he added, "I believe that man thus imitates God, who takes care for the well-being of the universe whether human beings recognize this or not."

Theory and Practice

Leibniz was never at home in the ivory tower of theory. In accordance with his fundamental conviction that the world is the best of all possible worlds because it is capable of being further perfected, he himself wanted to work for the benefit of society. He writes: "The art of practice is such that one brings chance itself under the yoke of science. The more one does this, the more does theory conform to practice."

Although one can scarcely summarize all of Leibniz' inventions and fields of activity, one instance will be helpful: When the first German scientific periodical appeared in Leipzig in 1682, it was thanks to Leibniz' contributions that within a short time, it did not fear comparison with the publications of the British Royal Society and the corresponding journal in France. A paper he wrote on quadrature of the circle appeared in the first issue; there followed contributions on optics,

---

2. Adapted from *The Political Economy of the American Revolution*, Nancy Spannaus and Christopher White, eds., 2nd edition, *EIR*, 1996, pp. 224-27.

Museum Schloss Herrenhausen

The calculating machine for the four basic mathematical operations developed by Leibniz.

chemistry, discount calculations, and many others on mathematics and physics, including the first publication of the infinitesimal calculus he had already developed in Paris, and expositions on the force/mass relationship.

Among the universal principles and their mathematical tools—with which Leibniz endowed mankind with far greater power over the hidden, *invisible* powers of nature—were the principle of Least Action, which Max Planck also used for his discoveries; the principle of Dynamics, called *vis viva* or living force; and the infinitesimal calculus. Also worthy of mention is the discovery of the dual counting system of binomial numbers, which opened the way to the development of computers. Leibniz himself invented a calculating machine for the four basic mathematical operations.

All this flowed into his plan to found academies of science in many countries. Such academies did indeed exist in France and England, supporting the scientists of those countries, but since Germany was splintered into a hundred fiefdoms and scarcely possessed its own language, Leibniz had to turn to the greatest royal houses. He viewed the purpose of the academies as—

unifying theory and practice, and not only art and science, but also country and people, agriculture, manufactures, and commerce; in one word, to improve the food supply, and beyond that, to make discoveries which spread the fulsome praise and honor of God, whose wonders would become better known than heretofore.

Leibniz found the final cause for applied science not in material things, but in metaphysics, that is, in the laws of a universal harmony which orders the material world and which the human mind can discover and make useful through hypotheses. "True faith is not only a matter of speaking, indeed not only a matter of thinking, but rather of conceiving in practice— that is, to act as if it were true." Thus science for him is serving God; as God, one understands the principle that constantly works toward its own higher development.

This vision of a fatherland, and Europe, blooming from the rubble of the Thirty Years' War, led him to many royal courts.

While at home in Hannover he served its prince as a confidential adviser and was the confidant of Princess Sophie. Leibniz spent three years, until 1711, in the service of the later queen, Sophie Charlotte of Prussia. He met with Austrian Emperor Leopold for the first time in Vienna in 1700, and from 1712 on had free access to the court there. In 1711 he met Tsar Peter the Great of Russia and proposed to the Tsar his program for comprehensive support of science. He made military-technical proposals, and got a promise from Peter for field measurements in the Russian Empire on the declination of the magnetic field, that is, how far it varies from true north. His influence extended to the court of the Emperor of China, in that the missionaries who were studying astronomy and other sciences with the Chinese Emperor received suggestions from Leibniz. Thus, for example, he proposed they make the Emperor a gift of Leibniz' calculating machine. After many unsuccessful efforts, he succeeded in founding the Academies of Berlin and St. Petersburg, which gave great stimulus to the development of these countries.

Dead or Living Matter?

Leibniz' "theory and practice" opened up great progress for mankind. For example, until that time mankind had only known of dead matter, which the study of "mechanics" sought to render useful. Since Archimedes, men had employed the lever, the inclined plane, and the winch, together with the wedge and the screw, to this end. Only the effect of the opposition of bodies was investigated, but not the impulse which triggered their motion. Laws were deduced from the observed behavior of bodies, strictly according to the empiricist method, which denied any knowledge other than that from the senses, and which persists today in the reverence for Aristotle, Isaac Newton, John Locke, René Descartes, and their successors.

But can the impulse, the reason for the observed motion, be detected by the senses at all? Above all René Descartes, who is still held to be a scientist, stands for the unreasoning nature of this thinking, describing bodies only by their mass and weight. For this he used the term "quantity of motion," meaning mass times velocity.

It follows from this that a ball with a mass of 1,000 kg and a velocity of 1 km/hr (quantity of motion 1,000), has the same impact as a ball weighing 1 kg and traveling at 1,000 km/hr (quantity of motion also 1,000). But the large ball of 1,000 kg and 1 km/hr velocity will be stopped by a wall which a cannonball of 1 kg at 1,000 km/hr can destroy. The same quantities of motion thus give different results in reality.

Leibniz, by contrast, compared the so-called kinetic energy possessed by a body weighing 1 kg which falls 4 meters, with the work by which a body weighing 4 kg is raised to a height of 1 meter. He used Galileo's laws of free fall for this purpose, and discovered the special proportionality between the distance fallen and the time required. He named this the "living force," the *vis viva* of the falling body. The velocity must be squared: This "living force" is equal to mass times velocity *squared*, and not simply mass times velocity, as Descartes and his school claimed.

Leibniz thus discovered new laws of motion, which he named the science of dynamics. It is concerned with invisible causes, which can nonetheless be proven experimentally, while mechanics had investigated only the visible effects for more than 2,000 years. His thinking turned toward the future result of work; it was necessary to measure the future *vis viva* of the motion. But this can only be done by the mind, so that Leibniz rightly called this force metaphysical, because it rules the visible from the invisible realm, and can be discovered and made useful only through the hypotheses of reason.

This had a great influence on the invention of the steam engine. His earlier acquaintance Denis Papin occupied himself intensively and successfully with this invention. In building the first precursor of the steam engine, Leibniz supported him in the attempt to concentrate the force of the steam. For in this way, the *vis viva* was able to unleash force, because the small steam particles produced more force as their velocity increased.

The competing English model, on the other hand, used only the counter-pressure of the atmosphere to run pumps with steam—for example, for pumping water out of mines. It would never have led to steamships or steam-powered vehicles, because the force was insufficient. Newton's Royal Society suppressed Papin and his invention, and thus set back the building of steamships and the industrial revolution powered by steam for a century.[3]

In his paper, *Specimen Dynamicum*, Leibniz brings his superior method to bear:

> Beyond the pure mathematical principles which belong to sense perceptions, one must also accept the metaphysical principles which are grasped only in thought ... It is of no consequence whether we designate this principle as form or power.

Can the Spirit of the Renaissance Be Revived Today?

Leibniz was intensely fascinated with the discovery of how creativity acts in living things and in the Cosmos, and how human beings can willfully control it. Human creativity was, for him, a natural law like gravitation or the principle of life. He astonished his age by spreading the idea of "Monads," initially described as "having no parts." For the quality of the One is a decisive characteristic of all creative discovery in Classical art and natural science.

Yet Leibniz stressed (in *Monadology* §10): "I consider it as a given that ... the created Monads underlie

---

3. http://schillerinstitute.org/educ/pedagogy/steam_engine.html

change, and that this change is continually occurring in every Monad…. The activity of their inner principle can be designated as striving."

Unity thus encompasses a continuous process, as a poem consists in strophes of different thoughts, whose unity is able to form the creative thought. The same occurs in Classical musical composition, where themes and variations aspire to a unity, as also in discovery in the natural sciences, in which the discovery process passes through many contradictions and paradoxes to the new unity or discovery.

According to Leibniz, Monads express through perception or cognition the entire universe from their viewpoint. Thus he compares Monads to the manifold perspectives under which a city can be seen from different standpoints. The *Metaphysical Disquisitions* says in §14 that Monads are the individual perspectives of the divine view of the world.

Lyndon LaRouche writes of this:

Thus, true science is not the mere observation and description of our experience of nature. Science properly comprehended, is also a centrally underlying principle of the cognitive powers which distinguish the creative scientific and artistic potential of the human mind from what might be described, loosely speaking, as the 'mental life' of the beasts. It is the crucial expression of that which distinguishes an actually human soul from the kind of mere opinion which is found among the beasts which we may have adopted as household pets. Thus, as I shall show in this reflection on my own experience, Leibniz did not exaggerate, either in placing the importance which he did on the role of the conception of the Monadology, or in denouncing the incompetence of the method of Sophistry employed by Descartes and by such followers of Descartes as the so-called Newtonians.[4]

But this idea threatened to bring down the entire system of tyranny which had destroyed the Italian Renaissance. Such systems are supported by priests and philosophers who tell the masses of people that the human being is only an intelligent animal, and fundamentally unable to know the secrets of the universe.

---

4. *EIR*, Feb. 22, 2008.

For this purpose the English monarchy called upon the Master of the Royal Mint, Isaac Newton; John Locke, the Secretary of the Board of Trade and Plantations; the philosopher David Hume; and the economist of the East India Company, Adam Smith. Their common foundation, their axiom, asserts that man knows only through the senses of hearing, sight, touch, smell, and taste, and that scientific knowledge is deduced from the combination of these sense perceptions. They admitted no causes in nature which could not be "taken hold of," and Isaac Newton, the icon of today's natural scientists, was supposed to have solved the problem of the attraction of masses by an apple falling on his head.

According to Adam Smith, the idol of today's economists, the individual does not need to concern himself at all with the consequences of his actions, a point which our economists today take very seriously. He writes in *The Theory of Moral Sentiments*:

Nature has directed us to the greater part of these by original and immediate instincts. Hunger, thirst, the passion which unites the two sexes, and the dread of pain, prompt us to apply those means for their own sakes, and without any consideration of their tendency to those beneficent ends which the great Director of nature intended to produce by them.

If the goal of the oligarchy and its Inquisition has been to raise beast-like subjects, the exclusive teaching of this ideology in universities and schools has today done the job completely. The spirit, the discerning soul, no longer has any place, and is even vilified, so that scarcely any revolutionary new knowledge is discovered—such as the planetary laws of Kepler, the Monads, or Einstein's Theory of Relativity—since now one is only permitted to draw deductions from given data. The creative idea is explained away as a phantasm in today's prevailing worldview. Men become mechanical, robot-like beings who run here and there, driven by their libidos, but whose drives can just as easily destroy them. They are not able to create a better future through the exercise of their reason.

Leibniz and the Fire of Discovery

Leibniz, by contrast, placed himself in the tradition of the great German astronomer Johannes Kepler (1571-1630) to defeat the barbarism of war and the stu-

FIGURE 1

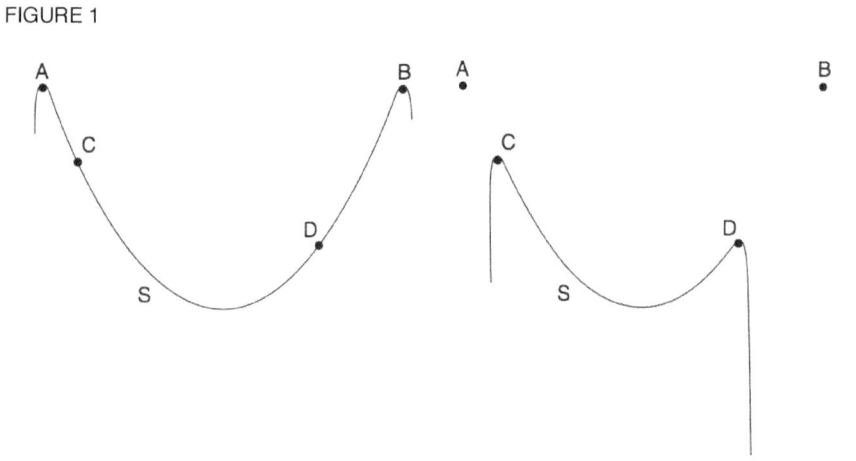

If one "disturbs" the equilibrium of a chain at any point and lifts it, it will always attempt to re-form a catenary shape.

pefaction of mankind. Kepler had already overthrown the entirety of the astronomy of the previous centuries by assuming a physically active cause in the Solar system.

Until then the movements of our planets had been explained only by approximations of geometry. Since Euclid (Third Century BC), it had also been believed that the smallest effect in the universe is a short-range effect along a straight line between two points—an idea which has still not been dispelled today. Yet the planets in the heavens move along non-uniform courses. They therefore cannot be described by calculations based on the circle, the dominant method in astronomy prior to Kepler. Moreover, the planets also change their velocity in a non-uniform manner along their orbits.

Kepler was able to solve this riddle because he assumed the causality of a dynamic, changing universe, which mankind—as a harmonic part of the whole through his God-given reason—could learn to understand. Kepler, and after him Leibniz, not only contributed to mankind's store of scientific knowledge in this way, but also redefined the role of mankind in the universe: The quality of reason enables the human mind to conceive principles that cannot be grasped by the senses, and to prove these principles experimentally through hypotheses. By mastering these principles, mankind is able to ensure its survival.

The anti-mathematical, anti-geometric—because physical—characteristics of the planetary motions are also exhibited by the "natural" catenary curve (see **Figure 1**) which the greatest mathematician of that time, Johann Bernoulli (1667-1748), and Leibniz had used for their solution to these natural phenomena. All readers are invited to explore for themselves the uncanny behavior of the catenary curve, using a free-hanging chain whose ends are attached to a wall or any other vertical surface. For example, if one "disturbs" the equilibrium at any point and lifts the chain, it will always attempt to re-form a catenary shape.

Why is this form constantly reproduced, entirely naturally—even independently of the material? How is this equilibrium and equal tension produced? What invisible principle rules each individual link of the chain? Whoever seeks to answer these questions encounters the nonlinear, almost living effect which our universe everywhere produces, and which bears a great similarity to the irregular, but nonetheless ordered motion of the planets. The question is also posed by the motion of light through increasingly dense media: How does the light beam know to bend along this non-mathematical path—what does it know, that we do not?

Many researchers have tried mathematically to comprehend the incalculable behavior of the catenary curve, thinking, as did Galileo Galilei, that it behaved like the geometrical parabola, which can be calculated by a mathematical formula. But nature does not allow it. This, also, reveals a defect in the ideas of the empiricists. Their research assumes only sense experiences and the mathematical expressions derived from them—and not reason. It follows the motto: "First come mathematics and geometry, then reality." This error is greatly amplified today by the development of computers.

Leibniz clearly disavowed this when he wrote, in a 1678 letter:

I rejoice in mathematics only insofar as I discover in it traces of the art of invention. I have cleared its hurdles by virtue of my love of metaphysics, for metaphysics is scarcely to be distinguished from the *art of invention* in general. For

FIGURE 2

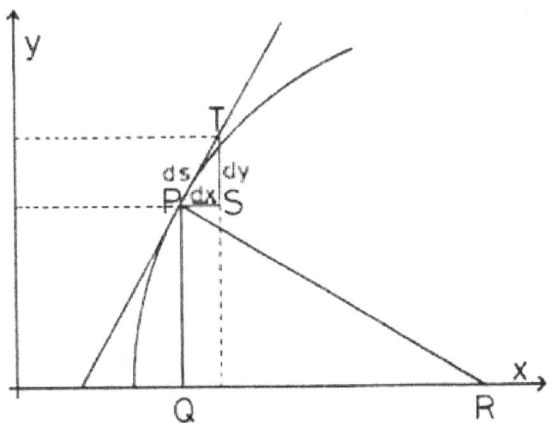

Illustration of differentials: The figure shows a circle to which a tangent is drawn at Point P. A right triangle is formed from QR, PR and PQ. The triangles PST and PQR are similar to one another; i.e., TS : SP = RQ : QP. Their ratio remains constant even when TS and SP go toward the infinitely small values dy and dx, and thus are thought of as infinitesimal quantities. But the ratio of the two segments dy and dx is precisely the sought-for slope of the tangent, and therefore a decisive quantity for the curve.

the idea of God includes absolute Being; i.e., also that which is in our thinking, from which everything that we think arises.

On the Path to a Solution

Thus Leibniz took the opposite path: Where mathematics cannot deal with reality, it is the mathematics that must be further developed. This led him to the integral and differential calculus. With Leibnizian thinking we can recognize the true origin of the integral and the differential, which our formal education has locked away from us in most cases. The scientist Bernoulli, who collaborated with Leibniz on the solution of this problem, called the catenary curve the integral, the expression of an active principle, and the smallest changes of the links, the differential. Both are shadows of an invisible physical process, just as the planetary orbits or the path of light through a medium of varying density are only shadows of their invisible cause.

Between a curve being investigated and a tangent at one of its points, triangles are constructed which become ever smaller, so-called differentials, which approach the infinitely small (see **Figure 2**). The differential calculus, based on this construction, was expressed by Leibniz in a formula, so that one could for the first time calculate precisely with infinitely small, invisible quantities, as also with the infinite. Bernoulli praised the method of Leibniz because it provided solutions which up to that time were considered impossible.

Yet from the beginning, a conflict raged around the understanding of this discovery, comparable to that around the understanding of the Monads. Are Monads the expression of continual change, which reflects the development of the Cosmos, or are they fixed, if also infinitely small things? No explanation is needed to understand that all empiricists—who recognize only objects of sense and accept no causes beyond the sensual world—misunderstand the infinitely small as a fixed quantity, instead of recognizing it as the shadow of a development, and they teach this even today in all schools and universities. We owe to LaRouche, who reintroduced the physical understanding of Leibniz, Einstein, and Max Planck, our ability to understand the calculus as the expression of the change in that process whose shadows we find in the sought-for change of the curve.

Leibniz had to defend himself against this misunderstanding, and rejected it energetically: "The infinitely small and large can always be viewed as arbitrarily small or large, so that the expression always designates only a "complete species," but not an individual "final member." Note that "complete species" presumes a non-sensual knowledge and cannot be any "thing" of the senses, so that here we are again reminded of the idea of the Monads.

This discovery made possible the calculation of motions of all kinds for the first time, and thus enormously expanded the power of humankind over nature. In this way, Leibniz solved the challenge of the catenary curve and of curves of all types. His method enabled, for example, the 24-year-old Carl Friedrich Gauss to discover the orbit of the asteroid Ceres in 1801, based on only three observations—it was being vainly sought by many researchers. Today we can track the heavenly bodies and our rockets in space very exactly in this manner, as demonstrated by the landing of the Philae probe on Comet Churyumov-Gerasimenko: It had traveled more than 6.4 billion kilometers, *en route* for 10 years, looping around other heavenly bodies.

Thus mankind obtained an influence upon the future, which is itself no object of the senses, but is determined by invisible causes which can be known by means of reason. Leibniz sees the future as determined by the infinite capacity for improvement of the universe, and not by the pushing and pulling of the tiniest atoms on the shortest straight lines, as the materialist standpoint predominantly represents it down to the present day. So it is not by chance that he quotes Plato's Socrates verbatim on this question.

He writes in *On the Principle of Continuity*:

Socrates commented admirably on this in Plato's dialogue *Phaedo*, when he took the field against the all too materialistic philosophers, who did recognize a principle of reason superior to that of matter, but did not avail themselves of it in the philosophical explication of the universe.

(The similarity to the teaching of our churches today is not accidental.)

What it indicates is that the *mind* orders everything for the best and that *it* is the cause of all things, ... whereas they would rather take hold of motion and collision of brute bodies [!], whereby they confuse the mere conditions and *instruments* with the true *cause*. (Emphasis added)

Leibniz writes further:

This is—says Socrates—as if one wanted to give an account of the fact that I am sitting here in prison and expecting the fatal cup, instead of fleeing, as I easily could have done—and said that this is happening thus because I had bones, sinews, and muscles and these were extended in such a way that I had to sit down. But those bones and muscles were in truth not here ... unless the mind had come to the decision that it were more worthy of Socrates to obey the law. This Platonic point deserves to be read in its entirety, because it contains fundamental and extraordinarily beautiful thoughts.

Leibniz unmistakably calls us to be ready to make even great sacrifices in the fight against the suppressors of truth and oppressors of mankind.

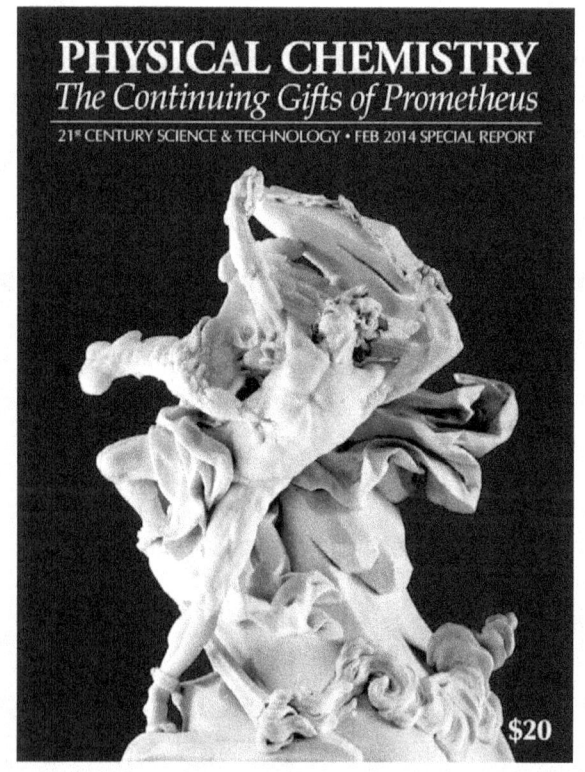

II. The Threat of War

Only a New Paradigm for U.S.-China Relations Can Prevent War

by William Jones

July 10—The issue of a "new paradigm" in international relations was broached by representatives from the Schiller Institute and *Executive Intelligence Review* (*EIR*) at an international press conference in Washington on July 6. Participating in a press conference in which leading Chinese scholars and U.S. scholars were discussing the burgeoning crisis in the South China Sea, a region where the United States has provocatively deployed warships, including two aircraft carriers, as a "show of muscle," Helga Zepp-LaRouche, the founder of the Schiller Institutes and William Jones, the *EIR* Washington Bureau Chief, put the issue of a "new paradigm" on the table in front of the assembled Chinese and other media gathered for the event.

Speaking to the participants from the floor, Zepp-LaRouche addressed her comments to Brendan Mulvaney, a professor at the U.S. Naval Academy and one of the American speakers:

My question is 'Can Mankind not rise to a higher level of cooperation and go for a New Paradigm where geopolitics is overcome and replaced by the commons aims of mankind?' The world is in dire need for the United States and China to work together, because I think without these two countries joining hands, the world is in trouble.

EIRNS

A press conference held in Washington, D.C. on July 6, 2016, sponsored by the Chongyang Institute for Financial Studies at Renmin University of China and the National Institute of South Sea Studies. From left: Zhu Feng, Executive Director, China Center for Collaborative Studies of the South China Sea, Nanjing University; Huang Renwei, Vice President, Shanghai Academy of Social Sciences; Wu Shicun, President, National Institute for South China Sea Studies; Wang Wen, Executive Dean, Chongyang Institute for Financial Studies, Renmin University; Brendan Mulvaney, a professor at the U.S. Naval Academy; and EIR Washington, D.C. Bureau Chief William Jones.

Founder of the Schiller Institutes Helga Zepp-LaRouche spoke to the participants of the press conference.

Dai Bingguo, a former State Councilor and high-level diplomat, spoke July 5, 2016, at the U.S.-China Dialogue on the South China Sea in Washington, D.C., cosponsored by the Carnegie Endowment for International Peace and Chongyang Institute for Financial Studies at Renmin University, in coordination with the National Institute for South China Sea Studies and Woodrow Wilson International Center for Scholars.

So the question is: 'Can the world move to a New Paradigm of peaceful cooperation for the future tasks of all of humanity?

Mulvaney, so typical of the "mainstream" view of U.S. defense intellectuals since the Obama "pivot," replied (not without a tint of cynicism) that he "was hopeful" that that might happen but that "the history of mankind of mankind doesn't bear that out." In response to Zepp-LaRouche's warnings of the danger of war, Mulvaney replied, that even if a crisis were to erupt it would be "small" and could be "contained." Such is that type of utopian thinking that has previously led us to two bloody wars in the last century.

Military Deployments Must Be Scaled Down

The press conference was the climax of an eleventh-hour mobilization by the Chinese side to ward off what could well become a major crisis when the Permanent Court of Arbitration on July 12 issues a ruling on a Philippine request regarding a number of issues related to the respective territorial claims of China and the Philippines in the South China Sea. Dai Bingguo, a former State Councilor in China's highest body, who headed the delegation and who, during his time in office, played the key role in top-level negotiations with the United States, delivered a significant speech on the topic of the South China Sea at the Carnegie Endowment for International Peace on July 5.

In his speech Dai warned about the "confrontational rhetoric" coming out of Washington and said that "heavy-handed intervention" of the United States in the South China Sea had to be "scaled down." While the United States is not a party to any of the territorial claims, it has leaned heavily on the side of the Philippines and has supported the unilateral decision of the Philippine Government to submit its request to the arbitration court in spite of a written commitment by the Philippines in 2002 to resolve the crisis through negotiation.

In addition, the United States has doubled up on its own "freedom of navigation" patrols in the region to underline its overriding presence there.

"How would you feel if you were Chinese and read in the newspapers or watched on TV, reports and footage about U.S. aircraft carriers, naval ships, and fighter jets flexing muscles right at your doorstep," Dai said, "and heard a senior U.S. military official telling the troops to be ready "to fight tonight"? "This is certainly not the way China and the United States should interact with each other," he said.

Dai warned that China would not simply sit idly by while such provocations were ratcheted up, as many in Washington are now urging them to do. "We in China will not be intimidated by the U.S. actions, not even if the United States sent all ten aircraft carriers to the South China Sea," Dai said. "Furthermore, U.S. intervention on the issue has led some countries to believe that the United States is on their side, and they stand to gain from the competition between major countries. As a result, we have seen more provocations from these countries, adding uncertainties and escalating tensions in the South China Sea." "The risk for the United States," Dai warned, "is that it may be dragged into trouble against its own will and pay an unexpectedly heavy price."

Viewing United States-China Relations Through a Telescope

Dai Bingguo underlined, however, that China wanted to work together with the United States on maritime issues, as well as in other arenas. "Even though the South China Sea is clearly not an issue between China and the United States, China is willing to maintain communication with the United States on maritime issues and work with the United States and all other parties to keep the situation under control, considering our shared interest in peace and stability in the Asia-Pacific," Dai said.

Dai also urged the new Philippine Government to withdraw its submission for arbitration. "What we need is not a microscope to enlarge our differences, but a telescope to look ahead and focus on cooperation," Dai said. "Both Chinese and Americans are great nations with insight and vision. As long as the two sides work for common interests, respect each other, treat each other as equals, have candid dialogue, and expand common ground, China and the United States will be able to manage differences and find the key to turning those issues into opportunities of working together."

United States Goading Its Allies

Dai's speech was followed by a discussion between experts on both sides. The visit had been sponsored by the Chongyang Institute for Financial Studies and the National Institute for South China Sea Studies, and their delegation included some of China's leading experts on the South China Sea issue.

Billed as the chief respondent to State Councilor Dai at the Carnegie event, former Deputy Secretary of State John Negroponte made his own remarks. While

CCTV

Former Deputy Secretary of State John Negroponte spoke at the U.S.-China Dialogue on the South China Sea in Washington, D.C.

reiterating the U.S. mantra that the South China Sea dispute "is not a bilateral dispute between China and the United States," he nevertheless supported the unilateral action by the Philippines to take the matter to the arbitration court rather than negotiate. "The United States has consistently encouraged participants to manage these issues "through negotiation and arbitration," Negroponte said.

But truth be told, one cannot see too much pressure having been put on the Aquino Government to sit down with China, which it never effectively did, but what advice the United States may have given the Aquino Government with regard to arbitration is anybody's guess.

Negroponte underlined, however, that the "United States considers a decision by the court a legally binding dispute resolution," i.e. when the decisions comes, you'd better follow it. Many legal scholars and nations, however, disagree with Negroponte on the "binding nature" of such a decision, especially given the manner in which the arbitration court has been brought in to decide on issues that significantly impinge on territorial claims, over which the court has no jurisdiction.

In private discussion during the following two days, the Chinese scholars made it clear that China was not prepared to back off from its territorial claims. "China doesn't want to lose any of its assets," one scholar commented. "Its two main concerns are safeguarding stability as well as safeguarding China's legitimate rights." Both of these have been subject to great misinterpretation in the U.S. media.

It was also clear in their discussions that freedom of navigation has never in a single instance been threatened, although the claim of such a "threat" has served the United States well in continuing its patrols to the "doorstep" of China.

Historical Claims Retain Their Relevance

EIRNS

EIR *Washington correspondent William Jones (center) and Helga Zepp-LaRouche (right) being interviewed at the July 6 press conference.*

The importance of China's historical claims was also underlined by the Chinese scholars. While the general attitude of the United States seems to be to ignore these claims in practice if not in words, yet for the China they are very important. And while the evidence for Chinese presence and administration on some of these islands goes back to the Han Dynasty, the post-World War II agreements by which Japan was to turn over the islands they had occupied during the war to China, were the key element.

As one scholar commented. "If you don't accept these historical rights, the Second World War becomes meaningless." Dai Bingguo himself had noted that even Douglas MacArthur was supportive of the return of the islands to the Republic of China.

But when John Foster Dulles took over the running of the San Francisco Treaty conference, Chinese possession of these islands was conveniently taken off the table. China has continually reiterated that its new role in the world after the long period of the containment of the Cold War, includes insuring fulfillment of the promises made in the post-World War II settlements, of which they were deprived because of the Cold War.

In addition to the private gathering at Carnegie, the Chinese delegation also held discussions with a group of U.S. scholars and diplomats pulled together by the Schiller Institute, in which the focus was rather on finding ways to overcome this crisis and finding ways to develop a more fruitful and comprehensive relationship between the United States and China.

At the press conference at the end of their visit on July 6, attended by some 50 or more press, the issue of creating a new paradigm in U.S.-China relations was put front and center. In addition to Mrs. Zepp-LaRouche's exchange with Brendan Mulvaney, it was also raised in the presentation of *EIR*'s Bill Jones, who was the other American on the panel. While criticizing the U.S. policy of treating China "as a predator even in its own region," he underlined the need for a new relationship, one that would greatly benefit the United States itself.

"The Belt and Road is the culmination of China's 'good neighbor policy'," Jones said, "offering hope and development to nations in the regions which are still plagued by poverty and underdevelopment. The United States has generally seen this initiative as motivated by hostile intent, in spite of the fact that the United States has itself been invited to participate in the Belt and Road and to work with China in building the needed infrastructure here as well. But the United States has not responded. This clearly indicates that we need a new paradigm in our relations with China," Jones said, "because if we continue with 'geopolitics,' it will inevitably lead to war."

Most of the coverage of the Dai Bingguo visit, which was extensive in the Chinese press, also highlighted Jones' comments on the war danger and the need for a new type of relationship with China.

The Onrushing Fall of the Anglo-Saudi Empire

by Jeffrey Steinberg

July 12—After decades of the most evil activities known to man, the Anglo-Saudi Empire is now on its last legs. There is no doubt that a confluence of major developments, some years in the making, have brought the British Empire and its Saudi Arabian partner to the brink of extinction. The question that is yet to be decided is whether the fall of this dynastic evil will occur through an orderly process, through actions by sovereign forces, largely aligned with the Eurasian powers—Russia, China and India—or whether they will bring down humanity with them, in their fall.

Beyond Rescue

The events that are at the root of this death knell for the British-Saudi Empire, have been grabbing international headlines for months. But it is the cumulative impact of those developments that has been willfully obscured by the mainstream English-language media:

• The recent Brexit vote, withdrawing the United Kingdom from the European Union by referendum, has unleashed a process of disintegration of the United Kingdom itself, with Scotland already planning its second referendum for independence from the UK, and with Northern Ireland moving towards its own referendum to join with Ireland and leave the UK as well. While the process will play out over months and perhaps years, the die has been cast.

• After years of delay, the Chilcot Commission report on the role of Tony Blair and his Cabinet in the rush to war in Iraq in 2003—in partnership with the George W. Bush government in the United States—was finally released early this month. It is a damning indictment of Blair, in particular, as a war criminal guilty of offensive war, in clear violation of the United Nations Charter. Blair is facing lawsuits by families of the British soldiers killed in that illegal war, and there are strong calls for Blair, Bush, Vice President Dick Cheney, Defense Secretary Donald Rumsfeld, and Deputy Defense Secretary Paul Wolfowitz to all be put on trial at the International Court of Justice in The Hague, just as the perpetrators of the war crimes in Rwanda and Kosovo were.

In the United States, longstanding efforts by the families and survivors of the Sept. 11, 2001 attacks—joined by former U.S. Senator Bob Graham and current Members of Congress Walter Jones, Stephen Lynch, and Thomas Massie—have reached a point at which the release of the 28-page final chapter of the 2002 Joint Con-

Hajor/CC BY-SA 3.0

The fallen colossus of Pharaoh Ramesses the Great (the "Ozymandias Colossus") in his mortuary temple (13th Century BC).

gressional Inquiry into 9/11—documenting the role of the Saudi Royal Family and the Saudi government in supporting the Al Qaeda terrorists—is now imminent.

At a Capitol Hill press conference on July 6, Representatives Lynch and Jones made clear that, one way or another—through Presidential or Congressional action, or through public disclosure on the floor of the House—the truth will come out. When the 28 pages are fully released to the American people, there will be an unstoppable demand for an investigation *de novo* into the worst terrorist crime committed on U.S. soil—and the Saudis and their British partners in the crime's "Al-Yamamah" offshore black funding will be in the dock.

• On July 12, the House Financial Services Committee issued a report of more than 200 pages exposing the role of the Obama Administration, including the Department of Justice, in blocking prosecution of top executives of HSBC (formerly the Hongkong and Shanghai Banking Corporation, of British Opium Wars infamy) for the crime of laundering billions of dollars in illegal drug profits for the Mexican and Colombian drug cartels. The same HSBC, according to a 2012 in-depth investigation by the Senate Permanent Investigations Subcommittee, laundered money to Al Qaeda and other jihadist groupings in partnership with leading Saudi Arabian banks.

• The Brexit vote has served as a trigger for an already simmering blowout of the entire trans-Atlantic financial system, a system run from the City of London and its Wall Street appendage. Not only are the Italian banks and "the world's most dangerous bank," Deutsche Bank, on the edge of collapse. The London real estate market is another giant bubble that is ready to burst, with some of the initial real estate investment funds facing investor runs and cancelled contracts.

Threat of Thermonuclear War

No empire has ever surrendered power graciously, or indeed without a ferocious fight. The Anglo-Saudi Empire is no exception. London and its pawn in the White House, President Barack Obama, have done everything in their power to create the circumstances for war against Russia and China. Obama and the now-defunct Cameron government in Britain drove the NATO decision to stage one provocation after another against Russia—starting with the 2013-2014 "color revolution" in Ukraine—including the decision last week to deploy NATO forces right up to Russia's borders in the Baltics states and Eastern Europe. The Obama Administration's deployment of a missile defense system in Europe is tantamount to a "dare" to Russia to join in a thermonuclear confrontation. Any such confrontation will necessarily pose an existential threat to mankind.

Russian President Vladimir Putin, however, is far too smart to be drawn into this trap. He has already engineered a series of flanking responses, particularly in Syria, that have added to the accelerating demise of the British and their henchmen.

At the just-concluded NATO heads of state summit in Warsaw, however, the number-one topic of discussion in the corridors was the fallout from the Brexit vote, which has tremendously weakened the British Crown and now threatens to trigger the break-up of the European Union altogether.

The weakening of the British-Saudi Empire forces, including their President Obama, poses serious dangers, but also provides a unique, historic opportunity to end the system of imperial control once and for all.

The fall of the House of Windsor, the fall of the House of Saud, and the end of the Obama presidency in the United States are all in sight. Sane people everywhere should celebrate, while remaining prepared and vigilant for the final swipe of the monster's tail.

Every Day Counts In Today's Showdown To Save Civilization

That's why you need EIR's **Daily Alert Service**, a strategic overview compiled with the input of Lyndon LaRouche, and delivered to your email 5 days a week.

For example: On Jan. 7, EIR's Daily Alert featured the British hand behind the pattern of global provocations toward war. Of special note is British Intelligence's role in instigating the Saudi Kingdom's attempt to set off a Sunni-Shia war. This religious war has been the intent of British strategy since the Blair-Bush attack on Iraq in 2003.

We also uniquely update you regularly on the progress toward the release of the suppressed 28 pages of the Congressional Inquiry on 9/11, which would expose the Saudi role.

Every edition highlights the reality of the impending financial crash/bail-in policies that would realize the British goal of mass depopulation.

This is intelligence you need to act on, if we are going to survive as a nation and a species. Can you really afford to be without it?

THURSDAY, JANUARY 7, 2016

Volume 2, Number 97

EIR Daily Alert Service

P.O. BOX 17390, WASHINGTON, DC 20041-0390

- British Crown Pushing War and Genocide in 2016
- Financial Mudslide Goes On; Monetarist Tyranny Gloats over Bail-Ins
- Moody's Downgrades Portugal's Novo Banco
- Puerto Rico's Default: It's Every Vulture for Himself
- Wide Glass-Steagall Debate Set Off Again by Sanders Speech
- MI6 Mouthpiece Evans-Pritchard Touts Persian Gulf Chaos
- North Korea Tests a Miniaturized Hydrogen Bomb
- Uighur Terrorists Found in Indonesia
- Foreign Investors Are Flocking In to China

EDITORIAL

British Crown Pushing War and Genocide in 2016

III. LaRouche's Laws

LaRouche's Four Laws Urgently Needed To Save the U.S. Space Program

by Kesha Rogers

July 12—Following this article, the reader will find Lyndon LaRouche's June, 2014 statement, "The Four New Laws to Save the U.S.A. Now! Not an Option: an Immediate Necessity." In Mr. LaRouche's pronouncement, he stresses that the only pathway out of the escalating global financial crisis and economic breakdown is through a return to the economic outlook of the "specific intent of the original U.S. Federal Constitution, as had been specified by U.S. Treasury Secretary Alexander Hamilton while he remained in office." The urgent necessity for the reprinting of this article at this time is highlighted by events of the past week, centered on the heightened danger of an imminent banking collapse in Europe, including the precarious position of Germany's Deutsche Bank.

The steps that Mr. LaRouche prescribes must be adopted at this time as a matter of policy, both in the United States as well as in Europe. The full discussion of these measures is to be found in the accompanying article. Here we will simply state that LaRouche insists that no economic recovery is possible unless the following four criteria are met:

1. The immediate re-enactment of the Glass-Steagall law instituted by U.S. President Franklin D. Roosevelt, without modification, as to principle of action.
2. A return to a system of top-down, and thoroughly defined as National Banking.
3. The deployment of a Federal Credit-system, to generate high-productivity trends in improvements of employment, to increase the physical-economic productivity, and the standard of living of the persons and households of the United States.
4. Adopt a Fusion-Driver "Crash Program." The essential distinction of man from all lower forms of life, hence, in practice, is that it presents the means for the perfection of the specifically affirmative aims and needs of human individual and social life.

Return to Real Economics

We must put an end to a culture of degeneracy and economic collapse which has been brought about under the murderous policies of the last two U.S. Presidential administrations of collectively Dick Cheney/George W. Bush and Barack Obama. The actual attack carried out on the physical U.S. economy by these two presidencies, is now most clearly expressed in the destructive policies of Obama to move to ultimately shut down our manned space program, exemplified by the elimination of the Constellation program in 2010, a program which had been established as part of a mission to return to the moon, including the development of a permanent base of operations for space travel from low earth orbit to the moon and other planetary bodies, such as Mars. In addition, the continued egregious cuts to fusion energy research under Obama are intended to keep society in a state of backwardness and to promote a system of zero-growth, and the bestialization of human society.

We are re-introducing LaRouche's Four Laws policy paper, with special emphasis on the fourth law, "Adopt a Fusion-Driver 'Crash Program,'" as this is integral with my campaign to revive the space program. As LaRouche stated in his policy document, "A Fusion economy, is the presently urgent next step, and standard, for man's gains of power within the Solar system, and, later, beyond."

As far back as the 1980's, LaRouche had defined a space program which would be the most important and efficient science driver program to develop the physical economy and productive potentials of the nation. This was presented in his 1986 paper "The Science and Technology Needed to Colonize Mars," and also in his popular video presentation of that program in "The Woman on Mars."

The development of space travel and colonization is the expression of a healthy human culture, which rejects a zero-growth society that confines humans to one planet, in a state of so-called limited existence. A fusion science-driver crash program is essential to increasing the powers of a society's productive abilities for progress, to an ever-higher level of per-capita existence. The revival of a clearly defined national mission for our space program, would lay the basis for the development of highly skilled productive work, which would produce net returns, not merely in monetary accounting terms, but in the *increase of the creative and productive powers of the human mind.* A system of federal credit, as defined in LaRouche's Third Law, will be absolutely required to invest in long-term capital improvements of the real economy, while the unleashing and rapid development of the space program will create powerful net returns through technological spin-offs, as we have witnessed under the Apollo program before.

Space Program Requires Fusion Power

Krafft Ehricke, a German-American space pioneer, and a collaborator of Lyndon LaRouche, made remarkable contributions to the creation of our space program and the development of the rockets and space craft that carried our astronauts to the moon. Ehricke was also very aware of the necessity for nuclear power and fusion energy as the basis for efficient space travel and colonization. He stated, "The universe is run by nuclear energy. Space will be conquered only by manned nuclear-powered vehicles. Planning anything else for the late 1960s is, in my opinion, flirting with obsolescence almost from the start...."

Ehricke's prophetic 1960 warning was absolutely correct. Today people are foolishly calling for manned flights to Mars using chemical propulsion — a dangerous proposal which would subject astronauts to the harmful zero-gravity and high-radiation environment of space for many months at a time. Advanced fusion propulsion could cut the trip down to weeks, or less, truly opening up the entire Solar System to mankind.

What has been demonstrated here in the presentation thus far, is the essential need for a fusion energy crash program, as defined in LaRouche's Four Laws program, as the basis for human progress, and the freeing of mankind from a state of lower forms of bestial existence, to reach mankind's fully human, creative potential, as defined as absolutely superior to that of all lower species. LaRouche presents this as:

The knowable measure, in principle, of the difference between man and all among the lower forms of life, is found in what has been usefully regarded as the naturally upward evolution of the human species, in contrast to all other known categories of living species. The standard of measurement of these compared relationships, is that mankind is enabled to evolve upward, and that categorically, by those voluntarily noëtic powers of the human individual will.

The stated program must be adopted immediately as the measure for improving the condition of life on the planet and beyond. We must define a new national and international economic platform that establishes peaceful cooperation among nations, and puts an end to the drive for war once and for all. This is clearly represented through the policies of space exploration now being defined by the nations of Russia and China, in cooperation with other nations. Most emphatically, it is China, in its course to develop spacecraft for landing on the far side of the moon, which represents a total shift of unlimited potential for the progress of mankind. We must move now to put forward this urgently needed program for development and cooperation, and end Obama's continued attack on human progress.

THE FOUR NEW LAWS TO SAVE THE U.S.A. NOW!

Not an Option: An Immediate Necessity

by Lyndon H. LaRouche, Jr.

June 10, 2014

The following statement is for immediate action by all associates in all regions of the National

Caucus of Labor Committees and its associated practice. The priority is assigned to all means and measures of public action, nationally and internationally, without reservation. That priority is existential for the policies of our republic, and for the general information of, and by all relevant circles world-wide, beginning this date of June 8, 2014.

1. The Fact of the Matter

The economy of the United States of America, and also that of the trans-Atlantic political-economic regions of the planet: are, now, under the immediate, mortal danger of a general, physical-economic, chain-reaction breakdown-crisis of that region of this planet as a whole. The name for that direct breakdown-crisis throughout those indicated regions of the planet, is the presently ongoing introduction of a general "Bail-in" action under the several, or more governments of that region: the effect on those regions, will be comparable to the physical-economic collapse of the post-"World War I" general collapse of the economy of the German Weimar Republic: but, this time, hitting, first, the entirety of the nation-state economies of the trans-Atlantic region, rather than some defeated economies within Europe. A chain-reaction collapse, to this effect, is already accelerating with an effect on the money-systems of the nations of that region. The present acceleration of a "Bail-in" policy throughout the trans-Atlantic region, as underway now, means mass-death suddenly hitting the populations of all nations within that trans-Atlantic region: whether directly, or by "overflow."

The effects of this already prepared action by the monetarist interests of that so-designated region, will, unless stopped virtually now, will produce, in effect, an accelerating rate of genocide throughout that indicated portion of the planet immediately, but, also, with catastrophic "side effects" of comparable significance in the Eurasian regions.

The Available Remedies

The only location for the immediately necessary action which could prevent such an immediate genocide throughout the trans-Atlantic sector of the planet, requires the U.S. Government's now immediate decision *to institute four specific, cardinal measures: measures which must be fully consistent with the specific intent of the original U.S. Federal Constitution*, as had been specified by U.S. Treasury Secretary Alexander Hamilton while he remained in office: (1) immediate re-enactment of the Glass-Steagall law instituted by

U.S. President Franklin D. Roosevelt, without modification, as to principle of action. (2) A return to a system of top-down, and thoroughly defined as National Banking.

The actually tested, successful model to be authorized is that which had been instituted, under the direction of the policies of national banking which had been actually, successfully installed under President Abraham Lincoln's superseding authority of a currency created by the Presidency of the United States (e.g. "Greenbacks"), as conducted as *a national banking-and-credit-system placed under the supervision of the Office of the Treasury Secretary of the United States.*

For the present circumstances, all other banking and currency policies, are to be superseded, or, simply, discontinued: as follows. Banks qualifying for operations under this provision, shall be assessed for their proven competence to operate as under the national authority for creating and composing the elements of this essential practice, which had been assigned, as by tradition, to the original office of Secretary of the U.S. Treasury under Alexander Hamilton. This means that the individual states of the United States are under national standards of practice, and, not any among the separate states of our nation.

(3) The purpose of the use of a Federal Credit-system, is to generate high-productivity trends in improvements of employment, with the accompanying intention, to increase the physical-economic productivity, and the standard of living of the persons and households of the United States. The creation of credit for the now urgently needed increase of the relative quality and quantity of productive employment, must be assured, this time, once more, as was done successfully under President Franklin D. Roosevelt, or by like standards of Federal practice used to create a general economic recovery of the nation, per capita, and for rate of net effects in productivity, and by reliance on the essential human principle, which distinguishes the human personality from the systemic characteristics of the lower forms of life: the net rate of increase of the energy-flux density of effective practice. This means intrinsically, a thoroughly scientific, rather than a merely mathematical one, and by the related increase of the effective energy-flux density per capita, and for the human population when considered as each and all as a whole. The ceaseless increase of the physical-productivity of employment, accompanied by its benefits for

the general welfare, are a principle of Federal law which must be a paramount standard of achievement of the nation and the individual.[1]

(4) "Adopt a Fusion-Driver 'Crash Program.'" The essential distinction of man from all lower forms of life, hence, in practice, is that it presents the means for the perfection of the specifically affirmative aims and needs of human individual and social life. Therefore: the subject of man in the process of creation, as an affirmative identification of an affirmative statement of an absolute state of nature, is a permitted form of expression. Principles of nature are either only affirmation, or they could not be affirmatively stated among civilized human minds.

Given the circumstances of the United States, in particular, since the assassinations of President John F. Kennedy, and his brother, Robert, the rapid increase required for even any recovery of the U.S. economy, since that time, requires nothing less than measures taken and executed by President Franklin D. Roosevelt during his actual term in office. The victims of the evil brought upon the United States and its population since the strange death of President Harding, under Presidents Calvin Coolidge and Herbert Hoover (like the terrible effects of the Bush-Cheney and Barack Obama administrations, presently) require remedies comparable to those of President Franklin Roosevelt while he were in office.

This means emergency relief measures, including sensible temporary recovery measures, required to stem the tide of death left by the Coolidge-Hoover regimes: measures required to preserve the dignity of what were otherwise the unemployed, while building up the most powerful economic and warfare capabilities assembled under the President Franklin Roosevelt Presidency for as long as he remained alive in office. This meant the mustering of the power of nuclear power, then, and means thermonuclear fusion now. Without that intent and its accomplishment, the population of the United States in particular, faces, now, immediately, the most monstrous disaster in its history to date. In

principle, without a Presidency suited to remove and dump the worst effects felt presently, those created presently by the Bush-Cheney and Obama Presidencies, the United States were soon finished, beginning with the mass-death of the U.S. population under the Obama Administration's recent and now accelerated policies of practice.

There are certain policies which are most notably required, on that account, now, as follows:

Vernadsky on Man & Creation

V.I. Vernadsky's systemic principle of human nature, is a universal principle, which is uniquely specific to the crucial factor of the existence of the human species. For example: "time" and "space" do not actually exist as a set of metrical principles of the Solar system; their only admissible employment is for purposes of communication is essentially nominal presumption. Since competent science for today can be expressed only in terms of the unique characteristic of the human species' role within the known aspects of the universe, the human principle is the only true principle known to us for practice: the notions of space and time are merely useful imageries:

Rather:

The essential characteristic of the human species, is its distinction from all other species of living processes: that, as a matter of principle, which is, rooted scientifically, for all competent modern science, on the foundations of the principles set forth by Filippo Brunelleschi (the discoverer of the ontological minimum), Nicholas of Cusa (the discovery of the ontological maximum), and the positive discovery by mankind, by Johannes Kepler, of a principle coincident with the perfected Classical human singing scale adopted by Kepler, and the elementary measure of the Solar System within the still larger universe of the Galaxy, and higher orders in the universe.

Or, similarly, later, the modern physical-scientific standard implicit in the argument of Bernhard Riemann, the actual minimum (echoing the principle of Brunelleschi), of Max Planck, the actual maximum of the present maximum, that of Albert Einstein; and, the relatively latest, consequent implications of the definition of human life by Vladimir Ivanovich Vernadsky. These values are, each relative absolutes of measure-

---

1. The substitution of "3. Cancel Green Policies ..." for the correct, "A Federal Credit-System," is a travesty against the principles of any actually scientific principle. Only affirmative identifications of "Science," could ever be allowed. Only, the previous title: "The Use of a Federal Credit System" is permitted. Eliminate all use of reference to "Green Policies": the very use of that latter reference, is a fraudulent representation.

ment of man's role within the knowledge of the universe.

This set of facts pertains to the inherent fraud of the merely mathematicians and the modernist "musical performers" since the standard of the relevant paragon for music, Johannes Brahms (prior to the degenerates, such as the merely mathematicians, such as David Hilbert and the true model for every modern Satan, such as Bertrand Russell, or Tony Blair).

The knowable measure, in principle, of the difference between man and all among the lower forms of life, is found in what has been usefully regarded as the naturally upward evolution of the human species, in contrast to all other known categories of living species. The standard of measurement of these compared relationships, is that mankind is enabled to evolve upward, and that categorically, by those voluntarily noëtic powers of the human individual will.

Except when mankind appears in a morally and physically degenerate state of behavior, such as within the cultures of the tyrants Zeus, the Roman Empire, and the British empire, presently: all actually sane cultures of mankind, have appeared, this far, in a certain fact of evolutionary progress from the quality of an inferior, to a superior species. This, when considered in terms of efficient effects, corresponds, within the domain of a living human practice of chemistry, to a form of systemic advances, even now leaps, in the chemical energy-flux density of society's increase of the effective energy-flux-density of scientific and comparable expressions of leaps in progress of the species itself: in short, a universal physical principle of human progress.

The healthy human culture, such as that of Christianity, if they warrant this affirmation of such a devotion, for example, represents a society which is increasing the powers of its productive abilities for progress, to an ever higher level of per-capita existence. The con-trary cases, "the so-called zero-growth" scourges, such as the current British empire are, systemically, a true model consistent with the tyrannies of a Zeus, or, a Roman Empire, or a British (better said) "brutish" empire, such as the types, for us in the United States, of the Bush-Cheney and Obama administrations, whose characteristic has been, concordant with that of such frankly Satanic models as that of Rome and the British empire presently, a shrinking human population of the planet, a population being degraded presently in respect to its intellectual and physical productivity, as under those U.S. Presidencies, most recently.

Chemistry: The Yardstick of History

We call it "chemistry." Mankind's progress, as measured rather simply as a species, is expressed typically in the rising power of the principle of human life, over the abilities of animal life generally, and relatively absolute superiority over the powers of non-living processes to achieve within mankind's willful intervention to that intended effect. *Progress exists so only under a continuing, progressive increase of the productive and related powers of the human species. That progress defines the absolute distinction of the human species from all others presently known to us. A government of people based on a policy of "zero-population growth and per capita standard of human life" is a moral, and practical abomination.*

Man is mankind's only true measure of the history of our Solar system, and what reposes within it. That is the same thing, as the most honored meaning and endless achievement of the human species, now within nearby Solar space, heading upward to mastery over the Sun and its Solar system, the one discovered (uniquely, as a matter of fact), by Johannes Kepler.

A Fusion economy, is the presently urgent next step, and standard, for man's gains of power within the Solar system, and, later, beyond.

IV. Berlin Schiller Institute Conference

A Common Future for Mankind and A Renaissance of Classical Culture

EIR's July 1 issue provided extensive coverage of the Schiller Institute's international conference held in Berlin, Germany, June 25-26, 2016. (We had further coverage July 8.) The full edited texts of five addresses and one discussion (all summarized in the July 1 *EIR*) are presented here. They are: the address of Dr. Ren Lin to Panel III on June 25; the discussion with Dr. Bouthaina Shaaban following her address to Panel III; the address of Talal Moualla to Panel III; the address of Fouad al-Ghaffari to Panel III, and those of Alain Gachet and Rainer Sandau to Panel IV, all on June 26.

REN LIN

'One Belt, One Road' in its World Context

Dr. Ren is an Assistant Professor in the Institute of World Economics and Politics at the Chinese Academy of Social Sciences (IWEP-CASS). Previously, she was a research fellow in the Global Economic and Strategic Center at IWEP-CASS. Dr. Ren has chaired a National Social Science Fund project on emerging countries' participation in global governance. Her research focuses on global governance, particularly BRICS and G20; nontraditional security issues such as cyber security; and European security and politics.

Schiller Institute President Helga Zepp-LaRouche introduced Dr. Ren as follows.

Helga Zepp-LaRouche: I just want to say a few words of introduction. This is the panel which will start tonight and continue tomorrow morning, and has many aspects, because it deals with the question of the New Silk Road, the "One Belt, One Road." I don't want to make a long speech, because we have a very important speaker from the Chinese CASS [Chinese Academy of Social Sciences], one of the leading think tanks of China, who is a researcher on the New Silk Road.

Let me just say in comment to what the last speaker from [Panel III] said: If Europe wants to survive the refugee crisis in any human way, that is, not with guns and boats, and shooting at refugees or making dirty deals with Turkey—such that Turkey does the dirty work for the EU—the only way is to expand the New Silk Road into Africa and into Southwest Asia with a real global approach of development. And that should be part of what should come out of this incredible transformation which we are experiencing right now.

So without any further ado, I want to give the floor to Dr. Ren Lin from Beijing.

Dr. Ren Lin: Firstly I want to deliver my sincere thanks to the Schiller Institute because it is this conference that brought me back to Berlin, of which I would say "*Berlin ist meine zweite Heimatstadt*" [Berlin is my home away from home]. Here it is close to my university, the Free University of Berlin, and I'm very happy here to give this speech on One Belt, One Road. And my next thanks would be delivered to the audience, because, even though it is too hot here, you listen carefully.

My background concerns globalization, economic integration, regional integration, as well as OBOR (One Belt, One Road). Every time I begin a presentation, I always like to share my research findings with my academic friends—that a moderate level of globalization and regionalization would benefit economic development. But yesterday, when I got off the plane, I heard that this word "Brexit" had succeeded, which gave me a great shock. It shocked me and surprised me, because I began to question whether or not my former research was wrong. This is somehow a new thing. Does it mean the recession of globalization? Does it mean that economic integration and collaboration are not the proper solution to the global challenges and the global issues that we are confronted with?

But today I want to again argue for economic integration such as OBOR, and I would like to argue for the significance of economic cooperation among countries, even though we are faced with the phenomenon of Brexit. It is easy to understand why countries seek integration, sometimes regional integration such as the EU; and sometimes integration in a group across countries, across regions, such as OBOR, One Belt, One Road. That is the fight against the stronger challenge brought by globalization. As well, it is still one part of globalization, I would say. It means a lot, especially for those countries that are less developed or in a serious economic crisis, to work collectively and regionally in a group. It protects them from stronger competitors outside, also from non-neutral rules, unfair rules and regulations. Therefore, the full focus would be, why economic integration such as One Belt, One Road and cooperation is important and necessary, and how to improve it, and coordinate it with globalization.

Nine World Challenges

Before making a further argument, I want to share with you the background information that we're confronted with today. Why do you need economic integration projects, initiatives like OBOR? And why do we need to work collectively and together? I have nine challenges that we're facing in this world. The first one is that a global economic downturn has appeared, as you know. It is necessary, not only for the emerging and developing countries, but also the developed ones, to work collectively, to work for new sources of economic growth. For some 50 years, trade has hardly been able to contribute to global economic growth; do we have other solutions? Not yet.

So the second problem that we're confronted with today, is that emergent and developing countries are still facing the problem of development. And they're still facing the problem of poverty reduction. So far as we know—it's already 2016—have the [UN] Millennium Development Goals already been fulfilled? Because it's already 2016. It's beyond 2015. So this is the second challenge, development programs to eliminate poverty.

The third challenge that I would cite, is that global financial risk could jeopardize regional financial and economic stability. Therefore, to work together as a group could enhance the capability to prevent those outside risks and harms brought about by globalization.

Then the fourth: What is the fourth problem we need to confront? The countries such as emerging and developing countries, still need to figure out how infrastructure construction could effectively serve cross-country interaction. To update infrastructure construction is also an emergent task for Europe as well. Do we have enough experience in this? Not yet.

The fifth problem, the fifth challenge is that sometimes trade deficits occur, and they sometimes discourage cooperation among neighboring countries. This might happen to China with other neighboring countries; this might also happen between Germany and other European member countries. Is there a solution for this? This is the fifth problem.

The sixth is that we still have many geopolitical security issues that need to be settled, that will always hinder trust-building and confidence-building, as well as the normal interaction among countries. This is the sixth problem: It's loss of certainty, a loss of stability in the world.

The seventh, what is the seventh? Structural reform is highly needed domestically for many countries. We need to better coordinate the distribution of industry. Some industries do not enjoy the advantage of the cost of labor. Do we have a better solution to the reconstruction of our industries?

The eighth is that we have many regional and partial crises and instabilities in some parts of the world, such as the regional crisis in the Middle East, such as the refugee crisis here in Europe and the Brexit, a new phenomenon as well.

The last but not least, is that it is also difficult to integrate the many regional and global institutions. We have many, many institutions, some bilateral, some multilateral, others regional, still others global. Sometimes I just want to say there are too many! How can we coordinate among all these institutions and make it all work more efficiently?

Beyond all these nine problems, nine challenges I have mentioned, there are still more. You could just brainstorm and figure out more. How can we deal with all these problems? How could we share our common experience and work together for a global solution instead of a unilateral solution?

Here I would like, for the second part, to indicate several countermeasures that we could put under the framework, or put under the content of OBOR/One Belt, One Road.

Countermeasures Through Cooperation

The first one is to solve development problems by effectively financing infrastructure construction—sustainable advancement which improves people's livelihood—this is the first solution. And the second one is to together look for new sources of economic development, such as infrastructure investment. But now experience-sharing is in high demand, such as how to effectively run an infrastructure investment project,— to share the better experience of some countries, maybe here in Europe, for example.

The third countermeasure is that regional and cross-regional financial cooperation is very important, and we need to set up crisis-prevention mechanisms. Information sharing is also in high demand. Then we need to figure out how to effectively run infrastructure investment projects with all these supporting measures.

The other thing I would like to mention is adjustments of global value chains: This is not only an academic term; it has a concrete content. It means looking for the right connective point, for example, to relocate part of the industry chain due to aging populations or other disadvantages, since other countries have demographic advantages. This is the fourth one.

The fifth countermeasure I would mention is mutual complementarity. I remember a maxim from Confucius. In Chinese, it is [recites in Chinese]. In English, it means, "If I am walking with two other men, each of them will serve as my teacher. I will pick out the good points of the one and imitate them, and the bad points of the other and correct them in myself." This is mutual complementarity.

What I would say here, is, for example, that Europe has more advantages in technology, such as clean-energy technology, and Europe has more experience with project financing, with sustainable financing, such as PPP—public-private partnerships to run infrastructure investment projects. For other sectors, such as the service sector, Europe has more experience; and moreover here in Germany, you have "Industry 4.0." China and some other Asian countries would like to discuss how to run an innovative plan.

The next one is, having noted that a trade deficit may be a problem, do we have countermeasures for it? I would say that we have established some special economic zones (SEZ) locally in target countries, and we can show the experience of SEZ operations, which can serve as one of the multiple ways to reduce a trade deficit, since the products produced in the SEZ could be exported to China, could be exported to Germany, and to the rest of the world. This is another countermeasure.

The next one is to coordinate domestic structural reforms between cooperating nations, and redistribute resources within the group to more fully exploit potential productivity.

The next countermeasure is that we need to avoid and fear non-mutual institutions, and create dialogues between newly established platforms such as the G-20, for example, and the established ones, such as the World Bank and IMF, and to achieve some coordination among all these institutions. And make them work together more efficiently, effectively.

The last countermeasure I want to mention is trust-building. The economy and the security mechanism is asymmetric. The lack of a security mechanism leads to the shortage of trust and confidence, which blocks the process of economic integration as well. Encourage initiatives of trust building such as the CICA in Asia, the summit of the Conference on Interaction and Confidence Building Measures in Asia.

Thus we have all these countermeasures. Group solutions and global solutions are generally welcomed, since to deal with global issues, global problems, we need a global solution instead of a unilateral one.

What China Is Doing

Then what has China delivered in recent years? As you might have seen, China has offered many public goods to global governance. And what are the Chinese measures to coordinate the large numbers of institutions, and to better encourage economic integration and global governance? Here's my personal response.

For the first one, the key word is "inclusive institution." We dislike any institution that excludes the others. Contrast the OBOR, or the AIIB. The Asian Infrastructure Investment Bank, proposed by China in 2013, officially opened in early 2016. It includes over 57 initial founding members, from Asia, Europe, Africa, America, and Oceania; it is devoted to further improving the existing global financial governance mechanism, and taking into account the financing needs of countries, such as developing countries. This is the first key word, "inclusive institution."

The next one, the second one, is "inclusive integration plan." In 2016, China entered the Thirteenth Five-Year Plan. The Thirteenth Five-Year Plan clearly put forward active participation in global economic governance, strengthening macroeconomic coordination, promoting financial security, economic stability and growth, promoting a balanced multilateral trade system, a "win-win" situation, as well as inclusive development. Accelerate implementation of the free trade zone strategy, promote regional comprehensive economic partnerships, agreements, negotiations, etc., such as the Regional Comprehensive Economic Partnership (RCEP) and the Free Trade Area of the Asia Pacific (FTAAP). This is the second thing that China has delivered.

The third is shaping an inclusive global agenda. We talk about global issues and global governance. Therefore we then need a global agenda. China serves as the president of the G20 Summit. The Seventh G20 Summit will be held in Hangzhou in September this year. And this summit has been characterized by Four "I"s. What are those Four "I"s? Innovative, the first one; Invigorated, the second one; Interconnected, the third one; Inclusive, the last one, which also would be and should be the whole spirit of the OBOR initiative. This applies in several areas: It involves the growth model of innovation; it enhances potential economic growth and improves global financial governance; it has increased focus on emerging and developing countries; it enhances the ability to resist risk; trade and investment contribute to global economic growth; and it gives attention to inclusive and interconnective development, as well as poverty elimination. All this content bears the spirit of inclusivity and interconnection.

My last point is that OBOR is an *initiative*. Why do we mention that it is an initiative? It is an initiative, because it is not a finalized plan, but an open project that opens more support and ideas. So global public goods are in high demand. Not only in China, but here: The countries in Europe, in America, and elsewhere, are all responsible for these global challenges that we're confronted with today. We need a global solution to deal with global issues and crises; no single country could exclude the others.

So, thank you to the Schiller Institute again, and thank you for this conference. I would like to encourage more comments and welcome any suggestions. Thanks.

Open Discussion with Dr. Bouthaina Shaaban of the Presidency of the Syrian Arab Republic

After delivering her statement to the conference by video (see EIR, July 1, page 45), Dr. Shaaban was able to connect to the conference by Skype video and engage in some discussion with the audience.

Hussein Askary: Now Dr. Shaaban is available for answering questions for a brief while. If anybody has a question they can come forward.

Question: Hello, Dr. Bouthaina, my name is Salah, I'm from Libya; I'm a journalist. I would sincerely like to have this opportunity to talk to you. I'm not

going to ask a question, I'm just going to give you some notes and some information about what happened in Libya that you might know more about than me; and maybe you can say something about it.

When the West and the United Nations decided to remove the Qaddafi regime, they applied democracy to Libya. And we had two elections, and in the second election the Muslim parties lost the elections. They won only 20% of the Parliament seats. As a result, they refused to give power to the new elected Parliament and they occupied Tripoli and started a civil war in Libya.

Then the United Nations forced the elected parliament to sit with the Islamic militias at a table of dialogue to agree about giving them half of the government. So, is that the democracy that the West and the United Nations want us to have? Is that the type of democracy, where the loser is able to take power by force, and force the elected, legitimate authority to sit with him in negotiations?

Askary: I think your point is clear. But do you have a question?

Question: I'm just giving her these notes; maybe she can give us more notes about this issue. And does Syria want this democracy? Thank you.

Dialogue of Cultures

Dr. Shaaban: Thank you very much for inviting me to be with you at this very important panel. I think what I heard now was an intervention, rather than a question. And I think I said in my paper that what we have to do, is try a dialogue with each other about all the issues, and to acknowledge each other's differences and cultures. And that's why I'm so glad to be with you at this very important gathering, to speak about the future world, to speak about the common future of mankind, and a Renaissance of Classical culture.

Yes, Syria wants democracy. But it wants a *Syrian* democracy. I think every country in the world wants democracy, but they want a democracy that's based on our identity, on our culture, on our principles, on our history, on our civilization. And it is not acceptable to have one-size-fits-all, as the Americans say. That we have a kind of a formula that should apply to all people.

However, the result of this attitude is proving to be dangerous, not only for our country, but for Western countries. Because there are people in Western countries who are watching and understanding what is happening. And unfortunately this kind of attitude is feeding extremism and racism.

And so we are looking for a world with no exceptionalism, for a world where we enjoy the differences with each other; that we love being together, but on the basis of respect and parity. Thank you.

Helga Zepp-LaRouche: Yes, hello. I want to thank you so much for your wonderful presentation. And I was very moved, as were many millions of people around the world, by the beautiful concert in Palmyra, which I think was the beginning of this intellectual and cultural dialogue on the Silk Road.

Dr. Shaaban: True.

Zepp-LaRouche: Yesterday we had a very beautiful "dialogue of civilizations" Classical concert, where we had Mozart's *Coronation Mass*; we had Bach; we had Chinese folk-songs; a Russian children's chorus. And if you have some time in the future, I would like you to look at that, because I think we need to turn this whole control of the media around, because we have not only Al-Jazeera and Al-Arabiya [TV networks], but we have the mainstream media in Europe and in the United States, who are part of this unipolar control.

But I think we should organize, maybe in some other country, a real conference for an international dialogue of civilizations, where each culture and each nation brings forward the best expression of what they have produced. And you mentioned the great role of Syria in the ancient Silk Road, which is absolutely true and fantastic, and which has to be made known! Because people don't know history.

So what I'm actually saying is, maybe we should consider how to organize a real — in Germany you would say, *Paukenschlag* [thunderbolt] — an international *Paukenschlag*, where we just outdo the enemy, by beauty, by joy, by love in bringing together such cultures, and then broadcast it with all the channels and TV, satellites all over the world, and win this war! [applause]

Dr. Shaaban: Thank you very much. And thank you for reminding me of what happened in Palmyra, after it was liberated from ISIS and from all the terrorists. President Putin and President Assad suggested having a cultural evening in Palmyra, and it was really, really heartening, to see Russian musicians and Syrian musicians a few days after the liberation of Palmyra, playing together: It was beautiful music from both sides. They were all human beings looking beautiful.

They all acknowledged each other as partners in defeating terrorism, in trying to create a base for a better future, for all humanity.

I totally agree with you that we should think of probably arranging a gathering, an event — you would be most welcome to do it in Palmyra! But probably in the Autumn or in the Spring, because now it's a little bit hot there. We need to raise our voices [applause] to build the bridges. We owe it to our children and our grandchildren, to create more bridges. And I feel that both our worlds, the Eastern and the Western worlds need a different way of thinking, need the way of thinking that is the theme of this conference, that we should all look at each other as human, that we should all be brothers and sisters, in common humanity. Thank you. [applause]

Question: I'm from Denmark and we are working in the Danish Schiller organization in Denmark. Our problem in Denmark is that we are censored. Anybody who tries to tell the other side of the story is censored in Denmark, and also sanctioned. And now, there's a new law, if somebody in Denmark travels to Syria, you risk getting two years in prison. Not if you're going through Turkey and to the rebels, or ISIS, but if you just travel normally, just as a tourist to Syria, you risk ending up in prison in Denmark.

My question is what could we do in Denmark, and also in the rest of Europe, to help get the Syrian information out to the public? Because I think we have the same problem in all of Europe; we are not allowed, the politicians are blocking the people, and the newspapers also. So what could we do, or how could we help more?

Western Attitude Must Change

Dr. Shaaban: I'm sorry, the sound was a little bit shaky. If I understand what you were asking, about how to get Syrian real information to Denmark? Did I get you right? Because the sound was not good on the Internet.

Question: The question was that the media are very controlled, and how could we get the message from Syria out in the world, as to what's really going on, because it's very controlled all over Europe. And people who want to travel to Syria from Denmark,— they can even end up in prison for two years, under law.

Dr. Shaaban: Yes. The problem is that right from the beginning, [there has been a blackout] on Syria, — you know this is the first time I've appeared with an audience in Europe, and I'm very happy to be appearing

with you. I appeared two times on television, but even when people in 2012 or 2013—when media people came to Syria, which was very rare, they would start with accusatory questions. "How do you stay with this terrible government? Why are you supporting a man who is killing his people?" So they were not coming here to know what is going on, or to hear or to listen to us, unfortunately.

I think we need, all of us, to resist this corporate media, and to find other ways of communication between us. Because it is actually widening the gap between our societies and between our countries. And what we need is more bridges. I consider this panel or this conference a way of brainstorming together. I consider it a first step, in order to try to find ways of establishing better ways of communication. And you will find in us very active and eager partners to do that. [applause] Thank you.

Question: Hello, Dr. Shaaban, I'm Christine Bierre from the Schiller Institute in Paris, and we have been fighting this ugly man [former Foreign Minister Laurent] Fabius for years. Now he's gone, but the French policies remain.

My question is at this point, the Western media say that there are two offensives in Syria. One by the West to take over the Jarablus corridor going up to Turkey; and the other one by the Russians, the Syrians, and the Iranians, to recover Raqqah. Is there any connection, any coordination between these two offensives? And if not, what is the West doing there, and what can we do to stop them?

Dr. Shaaban: If you are talking about Western forces that are in Syria, I can tell you the Americans, the British, and the German forces came to Syria without any coordination with the Syrian government, which is a violation of international law and of sovereignty of a nation that was one of the founders of the UN, that is, Syria.

While, by contrast, if you see that the Russians not only coordinated, but *we* asked—the Syrian government asked the Russians to come and help us in fighting terrorism with their air force, because our air force is not enough to go all over the country.

So that behavior of Western countries in Syria and towards Syria is far from respectful, and far from respecting the sovereignty of a nation. And actually, this is part of the problem, because what they call "moderate" opposition, is not an opposition; it's armed groups who are killing and butchering people! And for one year, now, the Russians have been trying to make the United States differentiate between Al-Nusra and ISIS on the one hand, and the so-called "moderate opposition" on the other; and until now, the Americans were not able to do that, because there's no difference, really, on the ground. What does it matter whether I'm killed by someone from Al-Nusra or by anybody who's carrying arms and belongs to Jaysh al-Islam or [other such groups]? They're all terrorist groups who are butchering people and destroying our country.

So I think the whole Western attitude toward the war on Syria needs to be reviewed, at least, if we want to reach a peaceful solution and if we want — which is more important — a common stand and common understanding to fight terrorism everywhere in the world, because terrorism is a threat, to all of us, wherever we might be. And it's feeding extremism, even in Western countries, and Western capitals. We are more than happy to share our experience and to dialogue with the world for the benefit of all humanity. And this is what Syria, the old civilization, ancient country, would love to do in the rest of the world, and *with* the rest of the world! Thank you. [applause]

The Bundestag Had No Clue

Question: [speaks in Arabic] I'm very sorry, I feel very, very sorry about the situation now in Syria, because me, I was 30 years ago a student in your beautiful country and I feel so sad about what's happened, really.

Dr. Shaaban: Thank you.

Question: And I hate these people, this barbarism; they will destroy all the Middle East, I'm sure. That's their planning. I don't know why, but it's what's happened. And me, I want to fight so that this will not happen, so that we can help you and the Syrian people. Thank you very much.

My question is, what do you think about German policy against your country? This is what's very interesting, because I work for German-Iraq relations.

Dr. Shaaban: Thank you very much for your passion towards my country. And I'm sure those who visited Syria before the war loved it, and I hope you will come, all of you, and visit Syria, after we put an end to this war together.

About German politics, the problem I think is German politics or Western politics, probably do not reflect the understanding of the people towards the conflict that is in our country. In fact, I was a little bit shocked to see that the German Parliament — I saw that on YouTube; I hope it is right — but I saw the interviews on YouTube, that the German Parliament voted to send military people to Syria, to send the army to Syria. And there was an interviewer who was interviewing members of Parliament after they had voted for sending soldiers to Syria. And he asked them, "Why are you sending the German army to Syria? Is it in support of President Assad? Or in support of Al-Nusra? Or Daesh, or in support of moderate opposition?"

And unfortunately, most of the MPs have *no clue* why they are sending this army to Syria! They have no clue who is who! And they were saying, "I'm sorry I have no idea, I can't answer this question."

And I mean, how — how do you vote to send your army to a foreign country, without knowing why are you sending it? Without knowing the reality on the ground, without knowing why you are costing your people, the taxpayer money in order to send your army to a foreign country? For us in Syria, we find this unbelievable, you know. Because we have such a big idea about Western governments and Western countries, and we think that they are all very well informed, they all do their job extremely well, and they don't vote unless they are absolutely certain of what they are voting on.

And so, this YouTube really shocked us. Unfortunately, this applies to many countries, who have no inkling of what's happening on the ground in Syria. All we are asking for, is to know what is *truly* happening, and to decide according to the facts, rather than according to all the propaganda circulated in the corporate media, which most of the time, is irrelevant to our reality, not only regarding this issue, but regarding many issues.

Imagine somebody like me, who has a PhD from England, who has had three books published in English, taught at American universities, and European universities, and I am accused of being a terrorist, not allowed to travel to Europe or the United States. [laughs] This tells you the judgment and the assessment of what's going on in our country.

Allow me to thank you again. I'm *very* happy to be able to share this gathering with you, and I hope I'll be able to host you in Syria for a bigger conference, and to continue our dialogue for a much better future for all humankind, that we all long for. Thank you very much. [sustained ovation]

TALAL MOUALLA

Repositioning of the Cultural Variable Towards a New Modern Cultural Approach

Talal Moualla sits on the Board of Trustees of the Syria Trust for Development, and is Executive director of "Syrian Cultural Heritage Transformation" project of the Syrian Ministry of Culture. He addressed the conference in Arabic, and Hussein Askary translated his remarks into English.

Welcome. It is difficult to speak now, after we have seen this film about Aleppo and its details, and the presentation of Dr. Bouthaina Shaaban. I am an artist, first and foremost. I am a researcher in modern aesthetics, and also an organizer of international artistic and cultural events.

I spent the last quarter century outside of Syria, but I returned with the outbreak of the war. The war started in a simple way, but it became more and more complicated, and the more complicated it got, the more I believed that I should stay and do something about it. [Applause.] And therefore, I work as an independent artist, a freelancer, and I am also acknowledged as an expert on heritage by UNESCO.

I never thought about talking about myself, because I always talk about others. My paintings and my writings were the expressions of myself. So, the more the crisis became complicated in Syria, the more my interest in public affairs of society increased.

Targeting Syria's Heritage and Culture

Inside Syria, we believe that there is a direct targeting of the country's heritage and culture. It is a terrorism that leads to the deconstruction of the society from inside. We, as intellectuals, believe that this terrorism that is targeting us has two sides. One is intellectual terrorism; the other is terrorism targeting morals and ethics in general.

I never thought that I would ever describe what I have witnessed and seen in this war. But it is obvious that my narration and my explanations are my creative tool to explain the situation—intellectual, cultural, and artistic creativity.

Participating with members of my society in re-establishing the cultural identity of our society is essential. It is a conflict that starts with searching for security, and ends with confronting terrorism. So, therefore, as intellectuals, whether we are inside Syria or outside Syria, we are endeavouring to present the role of Syria's culture and heritage in these meetings, that brings us together, and the institutions that help preserve the identity of our culture.

Terrorism targeted culture, first of all, in Syria, and you have seen a lot about that. And it also targeted the memory. Therefore, museums and archaeological sites were targeted and destroyed, and human beings were targeted and removed from their places with all their values—culture, traditions and norms and all else.

Of course, talking about politics is a long discussion, but what we have here is a political crisis which has implications for culture and every other aspect. It affects the identity, the belonging to society, and the communication in society.

More Creativity, Dialogue of Cultures

Therefore, as intellectuals, we believe that the only way we can deal with this problem, is to call for more creativity, artistic creativity and a dialogue of cultures, promotion of the creative activities of artists in society, and thinking wisely, to reconstruct the human being inside Syria. Mankind first, and the other issues come later.

The crisis in Syria is not a crisis of a state, as it is usually discussed. It is a crisis of a society which is used to producing culture and civilization for the whole world. We have many issues that need answers, but answering them also depends on the international community's position, and the public opinion and international organizations, and the law which has to promote and enhance the values of humanity.

We suffer from the mass exodus of intellectuals, and the dangers that result from that are many. Those who emigrate are the spirit of Syria, because culture was always the spirit of nations.

The Attack on Culture

Confronted by destruction of all the major features of culture in Syria, I saw that the burning of my atelier and the hundreds of paintings I had made, by those terrorists, does not mean anything, because the violent tendency of these terrorists is to implant the idea of the *use of violence*. Through their barbarism, they take the humanity out of human beings. In their attack on culture, they are very conscious of the fact that what they are doing is destroying the unity of society.

All nations have experienced wars. These are the moments of transformation for humanity. We all have to be optimistic, of course, if we believe that creativity always plays a key role in peace, establishing peace.

I thank the Schiller Institute for this invitation, and I give my special thanks to the venerable chairwoman of the institute, Mrs. Helga Zepp-LaRouche, and Mr. Ulf Sandmark, whom I met in Damascus, and Mr. Hussein Askary for helping me to convey my feelings to you. I leave you now, hoping to meet you once again, in my home country, Syria.

Thank you.

FOUAD AL-GHAFFARI

Confronting the Aggressor with Hope for the Future

Fouad al-Ghaffari is the Chairman of the Advisory Office for Coordination with the BRICS, Sanaa, Republic of Yemen. He addressed the conference by videotape from Yemen.

Dear Mrs. Helga Zepp-LaRouche, the honorable Chairwoman of the Schiller Institute and the New Silk Road Lady.

Dear Mr. Hussein Askary, Middle East Coordinator of the Schiller Institute.

Ladies and gentlemen, who are gathered in this conference in Berlin today.

It is a great pleasure for me speak in front of you, at least electronically, after having made many unsuccess-

ful efforts to join you in person. Our excuse is that the Anglo-Saudi war of aggression has made us prisoners inside our own country, Yemen. The other reason is that the political leadership here inside the country have failed to fully recognize what our Advisory Office for Coordination with the BRICS has achieved in terms of establishing a clear vision for a creative and productive credit system and building a future for the nation along the New Silk Road.

We were hoping that through attending your conference and meeting you, we would be able to learn firsthand about the idea of a national reconstruction bank, as it should be, to ensure a dignified life for the people and independence for the country. This would have sent a message to both enemies and friends, that Yemen can be a master of its financial and economic fate, even after 17 months of a war of aggression which was intended to be a collective mass-murder of our people.

Although I carry a great deal of pain in my heart for the absence of my team and myself from this conference, nonetheless, I carry a great deal of joy and gratitude from you and for you for the outstanding awareness achieved in my country about the New Silk Road and the World Land-Bridge, and the new economic system of the BRICS. All that was achieved through:

• Acquiring, through our Advisory Office, the rights to publish and distribute the Arabic version of the *EIR* special report *The New Silk Road Becomes the World Land-Bridge*, and printing one thousand copies for the Yemeni market.

• Completing the public reading of half of the report, in regular reading events each Tuesday in the Yemeni Center for Strategic Studies and Research, under the sponsorship of the Yemeni literary giant Dr. Abdul Aziz al-Mugalih, and with the participation of government agencies, civil-society organizations, and different social groups.

• Presenting our Advisory Office's vision in a special conference organized by the finance ministry, resulting in recommendations to the government to establish a special national commission for coordination with the BRICS, and the founding of a national reconstruction bank.

• Signing a special protocol with the agency for coordination with non-governmental organizations for child care, in order to produce and print a children's guide book for the New Silk Road Report.

• Signing a protocol between the ladies in our Advisory Office and the Yemeni Novelist Club to write literary works reflecting the message and spirit of the New Silk Road. These would be novels and stories expressing the commitment of the women and men of letters to the common good and dignified economic conditions for the people.

• Signing of a special protocol for producing a guideline for training youth, expressing the rights of the youth that have to be included in the National Dialog for Peace and Power-Sharing. It will also in-

clude the outcomes of the first BRICS Youth Summit held in 2014, and in anticipation of the outcome of the upcoming BRICS Youth Summit in Ufa, Russia. It will also include the legacy of the Chinese new Foreign Policy Paper on the Arab World, which was issued in January 2016, and UN Security Council Resolution 2250 which is related to youth and peace and security. All these are to be included in our vision for a national youth policy.

• Our Advisory Office presented an offer to the Electricity and Power Ministry for a new power policy in the short term and long term, including the revival of our countrys nuclear power program.

• Establishing a website for our Advisory Office. (www.alfouadsolutions.com)

• Informing the different government institutions on the importance and necessity of preparing a special report for reconstruction of the Yemeni economy to be added to the Special Report on the New Silk Road, because this will strengthen Yemen's position in international negotiations, and will identify the true friend from the false ones.

• The Advisory Office paid special attention to the refugee crisis, and came up with the vision that large scale infrastructure and technological development will contribute greatly to this issue as they provide a higher standard of living to ever larger numbers of people.

• Training the members of the Advisory Office in reading the *EIR* Special Report on the New Silk Road.

• And finally, our Advisory Office has recently adopted a special vision for the inclusion of space technology and space science in its activities, to keep up with the developments of the New Silk Road in space.

All these efforts and achievements, ladies and gentlemen, were made in a record time of four months, under the worst military attack on our nation in known history. This was possible due to the dedication and resilience of the young women and men in our Advisory Office, who confronted the aggressors by creating hope for the future, and broke up with the conventional thinking methods to make breakthroughs that lead all the way to the far side of the Moon.

I thank you for your attention, and would like to send to you all a fragrant greeting from my homeland and its people, who are in need for your solidarity. We wish your conference all the success in its proceedings. We will hopefully be able to join you in new events in the near future.

ALAIN GACHET

How New Space Technologies Can Change The Groundwater Geopolitical Balance

Geologist Alain Gachet is Chairman of Radar Technologies International, based in France, which specializes in radar technologies in oil and water research. His presentation included detailed information from his case studies of Kenya and Iraq.

Good afternoon. I am not involved in politics at all. I am just a scientist. And I'm going to tell you a very strange story, a true story that happened to me, which started at most 15 years ago.

You know all these figures: 1.1 billion people don't have access to clean water today, and 5.3 billion people, two-thirds of the world's population, will be living in an area of severe water stress by 2050. You have heard of climate change; is that something new? We can feel it very seriously today. All the water tables in the world are regressing, going lower and lower, and we have a fantastically growing population.

So climate change and growing population means rising water demand and shrinking water supply. This figure is something that humanity has never seen before, has never experienced before. During the beginning of humanity, there were roughly 5 million persons 10,000 years before Christ, growing, after the invention of agriculture, to 250 million people, around Jesus Christ's period. Then, suddenly, just at the end of the 19th Century, we had a sharp rise which has no precedent in the history of mankind. How are we going to deal with that?

Converting Difficulties into Opportunities

It's a kind of paradigm that the Schiller Institute likes. We're going to see what we can do, because the key to human evolution is to convert difficulties into opportunities. We are extremely fortunate because, according to the computation of NASA since they have been observing the Earth by satellite during these last 30 years, they've understood that all the water consumed by human beings until now is this little bubble. **Slide 1** It means humanity has been developing on lakes and rivers mainly, but the real bulk of fresh water is below the surface of the Earth, is underground. And it is 33 times *bigger*, than all the water quantities we have been consuming up to now. So that's a great good fortune for the future of humanity. This is water for the future.

But where and how to find it, that is the challenge.

In fact, I am from the oil industry. I have nothing to do with water. You know, water is not quoted on the stock market; water has no value, except when you die of thirst. It's what I understood is my job.

Discovering Water

So, I was working for an oil exploration project for Shell in the desert of Libya, when I discovered—this is the desert of Libya—when I discovered on the same

SLIDE 1

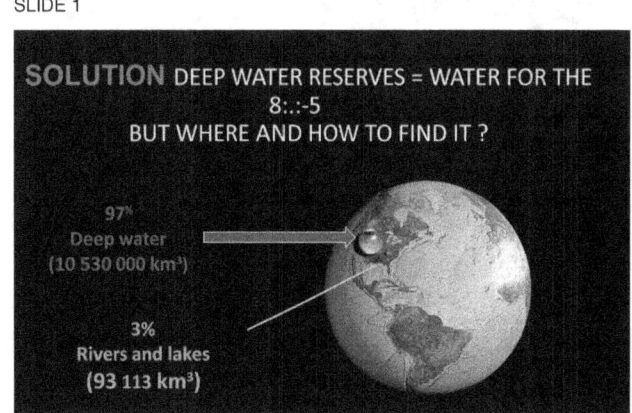

SLIDE 2

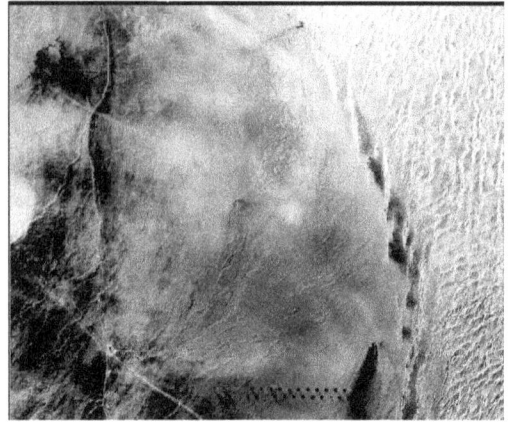

SLIDE 3

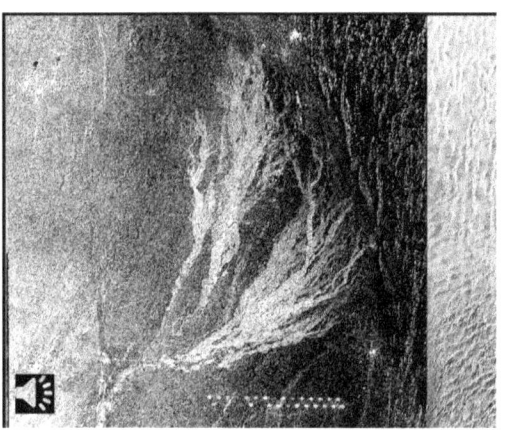

SLIDE 4

image, using radar,— this is optical **Slide 2**, this is radar **Slide 3**. From 800 km altitude, I discovered this monster. It's a monster.

Using radar, we know that radar is sensitive to moisture, soil moisture and surface roughness. This is surface roughness which is bright, but this brightness is a response from a big leakage of water coming from a big

SLIDE 5

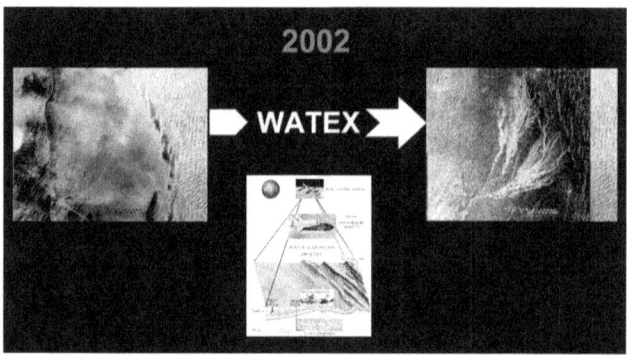

SLIDE 6

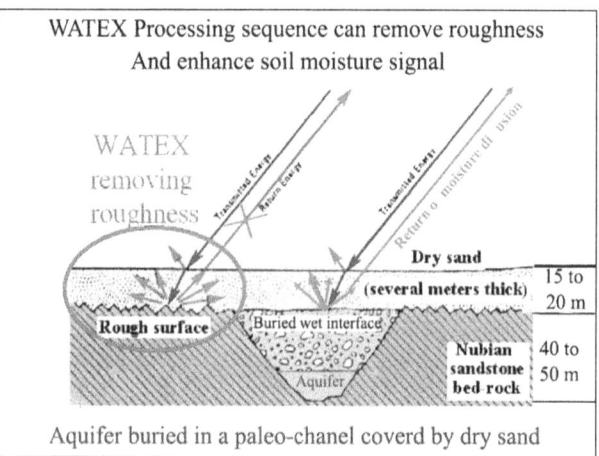

pipeline. This is the result of the Great Man-Made River created by Qaddafi several years ago. This was a big project and the leakage occurred somewhere here. So it was a pure accident, in my oil exploration program, that I discovered this image.

So it gave me the idea—this is the size of the pipe **Slide 4**—it gave me the idea of finding water, underground water, using radar; just a simple idea, just from an accident. But the main problem is jumping from an optical image to radar image. Yes, so we need radar to find water underground. But on this image you have two effects, the effects on the surface—roughness means rocks, boulders, all houses and metallic pieces such as rooftops and so on—and moisture. **Slide 5** The main goal is to get rid of the surface obstacles, to pinpoint only moisture, in order to be able detect something deeper. That was a real challenge: combining images from space, geophysics, geology, and whatever we know from the Earth, and first eliminating the roughness effect by a special mathematical algorithm, just to maintain the response of humidity here, **Slide 6** leading to an aquifer which is deeper.

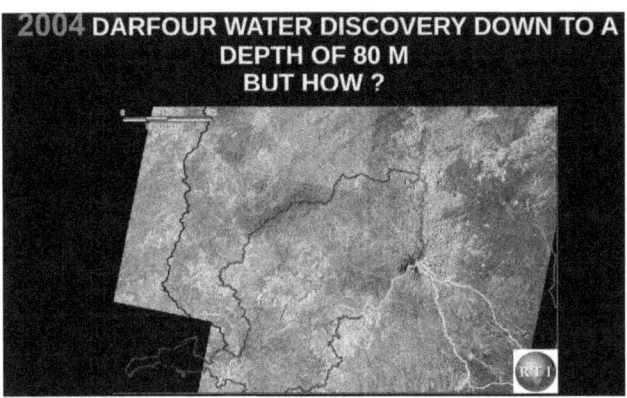

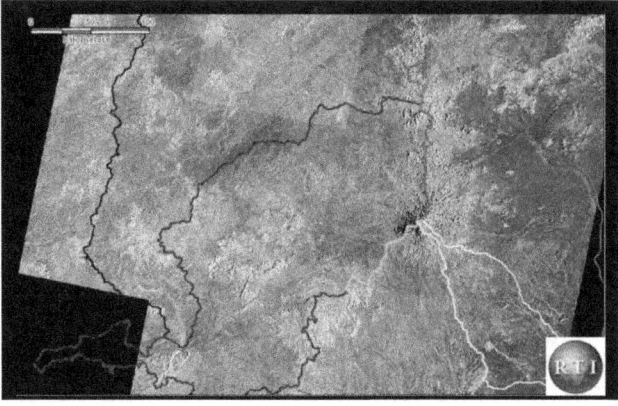

Sudan Crisis

This took me two years of intensive work, and when the algorithm had been invented, a few weeks later, the Darfur crisis broke out, in February 2004. So I was called by the UNHCR in Geneva, because they knew about the work I was doing, and they told me, "Alain, we have something like 250,000 people fleeing Sudan, and we tried to put them in camps; we spent millions of dollars to truck water to these refugees. Can you help us find water?" I said, "I don't know. I never experienced it; I just now invented the system. Let's see from today: we are going to jump from the desk to the ground, and to see if we can do something."

So this is a radar image that everybody can have, of all Sudan; this is all Darfur **Slide 7**. Look at the scale here, it's a big area, 400 km by almost 400 km here, so it's 200,000 square km. We have 3 million displaced persons in camps, what can we do to help them? The system allowed me to jump from this **Slide 8** image, to *this* image **Slide 9**—it's exactly the same; we jump from this image to *this* image, now we see 20 meters underground, by this special filtering algorithm, and we see a broad network of underground rivers, and if they're bright, it means that water is there; moisture is there, moisture indicates a big water system working underground.

So, we cannot let these people die of thirst, when we see such beautiful things. But now we have to prove it on the ground. And when you land on the ground, you completely change your life. You become a refugee yourself. You know, no protection; you're exposed to any kind of threat. It's a completely different atmosphere, I would say. And of course, you are exposed to dangers, permanently exposed to dangers. I was protected by the UN peacekeeping forces, and for only one

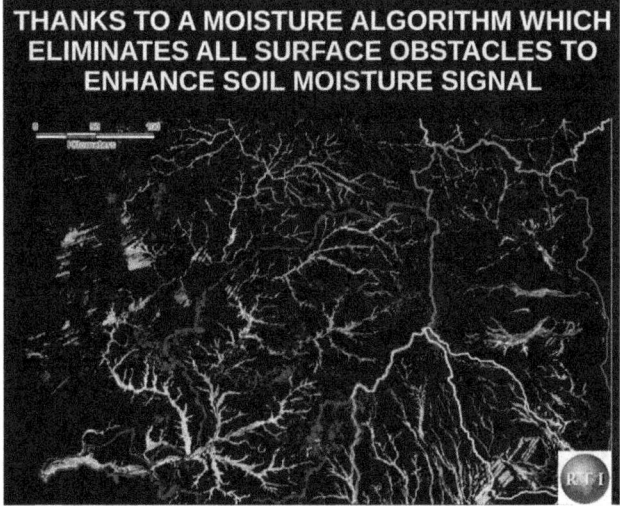

guy they had to deploy this whole armada. **Slide 10** The result: 1,700 wells have been drilled in two years. We have a success rate jumping from 33% to 98%, enough

2011 : HELL IN NORTH KENYA STRUCK BY DROUGHT

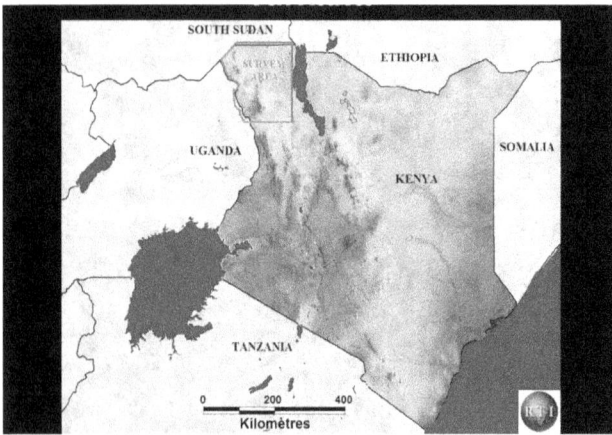

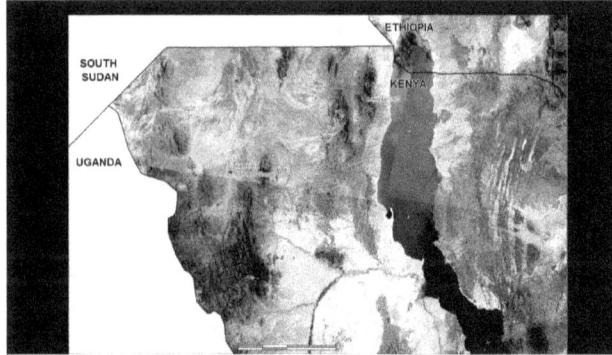

water to serve 33 million people, not only 3 million, but 33 million, and we saved half a billion U.S. dollars in water trucking. [Applause]

I must tell you, this is the result of a dream. Once I saw this leakage in Libya, I thought to myself, "If you

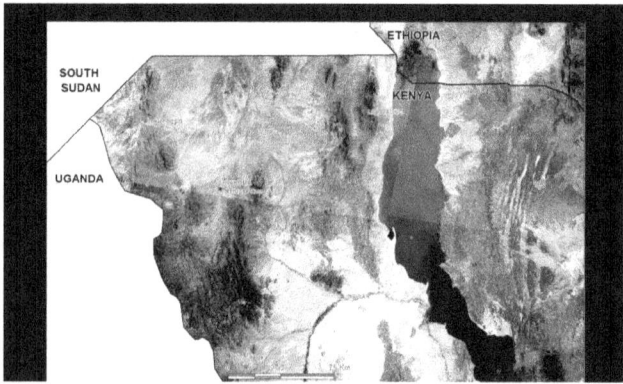

can solve the issue of removing all surface obstacles to detect only moisture effects, you cross a kind of gate, you cross a curtain, and you discover another world on the other side."

Horn of Africa Drought

I was more and more involved in water, and especially again, in 2011. A very, very bad drought struck the Horn of Africa, affecting 33 million persons, between Ethiopia, Kenya, and Somalia. **Slide 11** I must say, that just before, in 2007, the same drought affected the northern part of Syria, destroying the economies, destroying the cattle, destroying the crops, impoverishing the people, that trudged to the cities to try to find a solution. That was the beginning of the Arab Spring, probably linked to these phenomena.

But this massive, massive drought, it was really Hell, and I arrived just a few months later to map the geology of this area to try to find water. It was in this area, near South Sudan, Ethiopia, Uganda, and Kenya, what we call the Turkana area. **Slide 12** Again, a very desperate situation, and when I was asked to try to find water there, I was desperate. Look at this image: **Slide 13** Everything is dark, absolutely no water. The water here is brackish.

Now, to find water there: You have a big refugee camp called Kakuma, with almost 200,000 persons today. First we had ensure that there was enough water for them, so I have to map the geology of this area to prove to the UN that the Kakuma refugee camp could have enough water. That's the first case. But when I covered all of that, I discovered something much more important than the refugees of Kakuma. First, I jump from this image **Slide 14**, this is an optical image, I jump from the specially processed image, removing

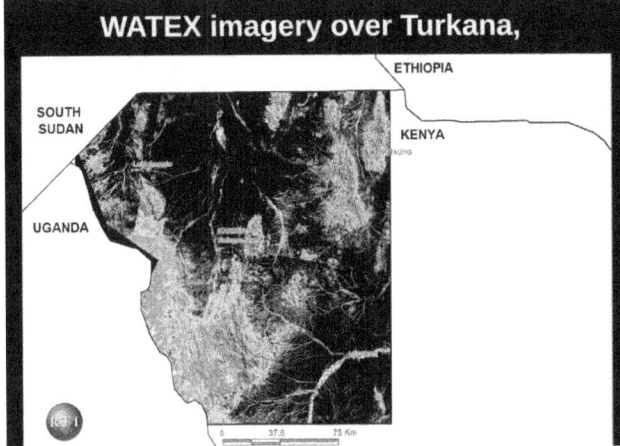

WATEX imagery over Turkana,

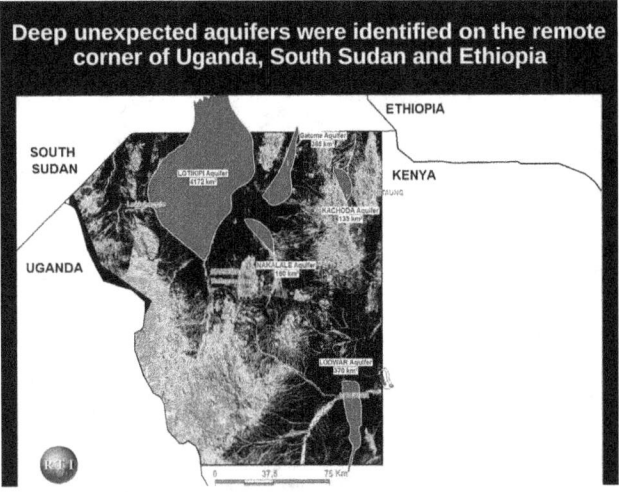

Deep unexpected aquifers were identified on the remote corner of Uganda, South Sudan and Ethiopia

Under the vast emptiness of the Lotikipi plain without a village on a radius of 50 km

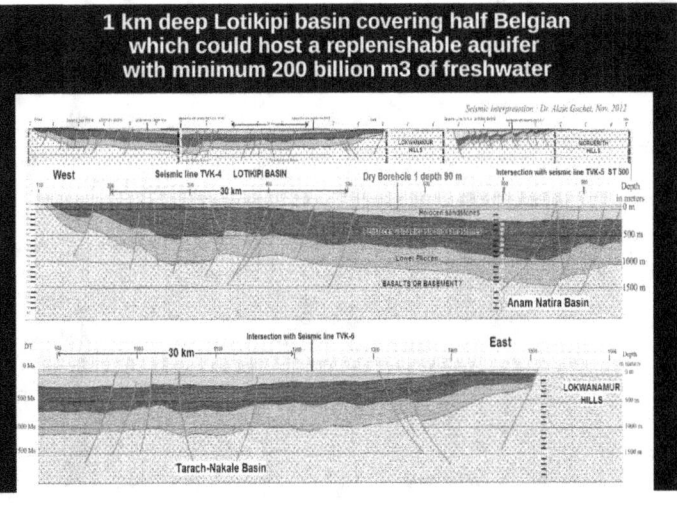

1 km deep Lotikipi basin covering half Belgian which could host a replenishable aquifer with minimum 200 billion m3 of freshwater

roughness, **Slide 15** and we discover black holes. When we see black holes, it's a good sign. It means that water is so deep. Water is coming there, and it vanished somewhere in the middle. It means it has been absorbed underground.

Water from the Desert

This could offer us opportunities of finding deep water, and the deep water, using geophysics and other geological data—we could convert this image, into this one: five big targets. **Slide 16** Just targets, it's a concept. Using this technology we derived a concept. This area is half the size of Belgium. Never drilled, never drilled! Never drilled. Near Lodwar, the capital of Turkana, probably something like 200 *billion* cubic meters, twice the size of Lac Leman in Geneva. Never drilled! It looks like that, very, very much like a desert. **Slide 17** And when I asked to drill there, the UN told me "Alain, you are crazy." I told them, "Yes, I may be crazy, but this dream, if we find water it will completely change the game in the area." So we have to go ahead.

Surprise, the cost would be the price of one well, one well down to 400 meters—this is deep water. And I had some echographies from oil companies; the fact that I had been working in oil was very helpful. From these seismic cross-sections **Slide 18**, I had the conviction that there was the potential to store underground water there, combined with the black holes of the radar image. And I found the water! It was there! [applause] *200 billion* cubic meters of freshwater were waiting for us.

Lodwar

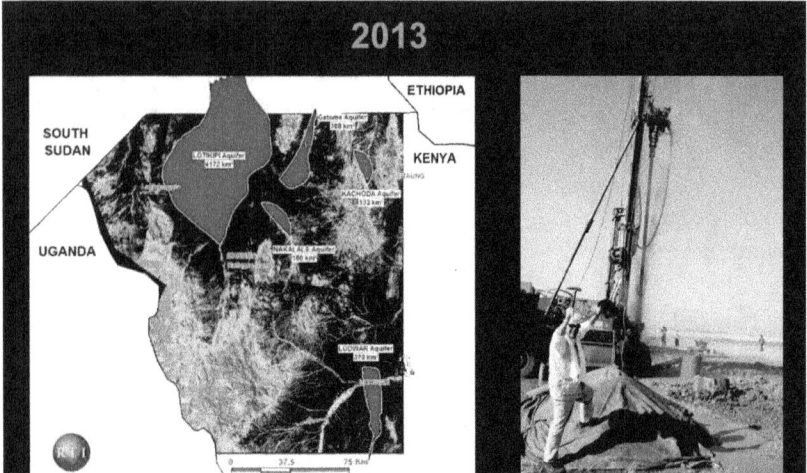

These women had to walk *40 km* every day to feed their cattle, to feed their kids. And *brackish* water! Now, under these immensities, where I was called a crazy guy to drill, there is serious, very important potential.

Lodwar

Now, let's go around Lodwar, the capital of Turkana, **Slide 19** hosting 10,000 persons and the capital of poverty, capital of dirt, where women were scavenging in trash at the town entrance to find food to feed their kids! I discovered, Lodwar is here, the big structure, a black hole, but to drill here—only 5 km from town! **Slide 20** Nobody had the idea to shift, and to drill there down to 100 or 200 meters!

Next one: The seismic, again gave me a very important trough **Slide 21**, where a lot of water could be stored, something like 10-12 billion cubic meters of freshwater, down to a depth of 200 meters only. The basin is 4 km deep, so it gives you a very, very important potential. And water was there again. These children have never seen freshwater in their life! Never!

Now, we have jumped from Hell to prosperity. **Slide 22** The women that were scavenging in the trash, now they have their own lot, they can feed their children, and this water restores their dignity. They now have animals, they can feed animals, they get milk from the goats. Now they can save their families.

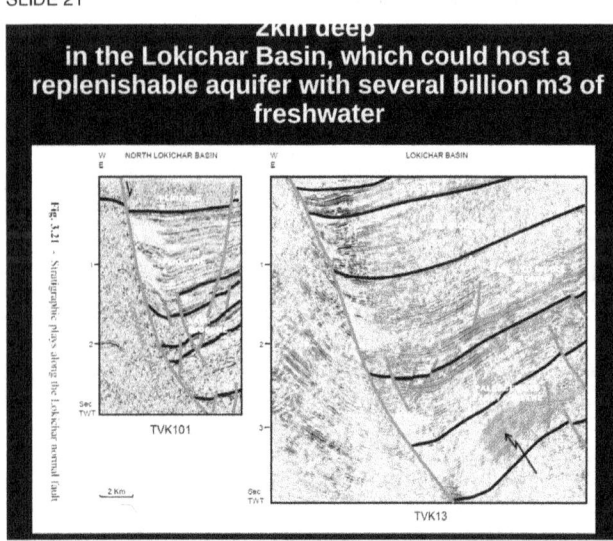

They don't need any kind of international assistance. The government now has to just pay enough for a well, to produce the wealth. The wealth is there, underground. And it is *massive*! This wealth is massive, and this water is replenishable, which is very, very important. All of that is replenishable resources.

Iraq

Last chapter: Iraq, the most difficult part. I started to discuss with the Iraqi authorities five years ago, during the time of [Prime Minister Nouri] Al Maliki. The water program in Iraq has been funded by the European Union under UNESCO leadership, and operated by my company. **Slide 23**

So, we decided to cover *all* Iraq. It's not a small part, like Turkana. Now, all Iraq, I must say, it was a big piece to swallow. **Slide 24** A lot of pixels: You know, each pixel covering Iraq is 6.5 meters, so we have an extremely high resolution of all Iraq.

As I told you, radar is very sensitive to roughness. Here is the roughness of the rooftops of Baghdad, Mosul, Irbil, Sulaymaniyah, Anbar, Rutbah; and here down, you see here the Euphrates, the Tigris—it's a mixture of roughness and moisture. Now, let us remove the roughness, just to see what the state of moisture of all Iraq is. **Slide 25** Here we are: It's a kind of image that you have never seen before; it's completely new. It means that now, you see the moisture, the soil moisture content of *all* Iraq, down to 20 meters. There are many consequences: first, the immediate one: if you want to plant trees, if you want to restore vegetation, never go in the black areas! Because the black means the water is deeper than 20 meters, so the roots of the tree will never reach any water—unless you feed them. You see the Tigris and Euphrates, they look ridiculous. They look ridiculous, because the dams in Turkey have cut off the water supply! But look at that: Kurdistan. *And* we could extend it to Syria! I don't have the budget to do that, but imagine what you have in Syria. Imagine that!

Al-Anbar, completely desert! I'm sorry, it's not that much desert; there are some kinds of patches of humidity. So we are still trying to understand where this humidity comes from, because it doesn't come from rivers; rivers have never flowed here. It comes from underground, very deep underground.

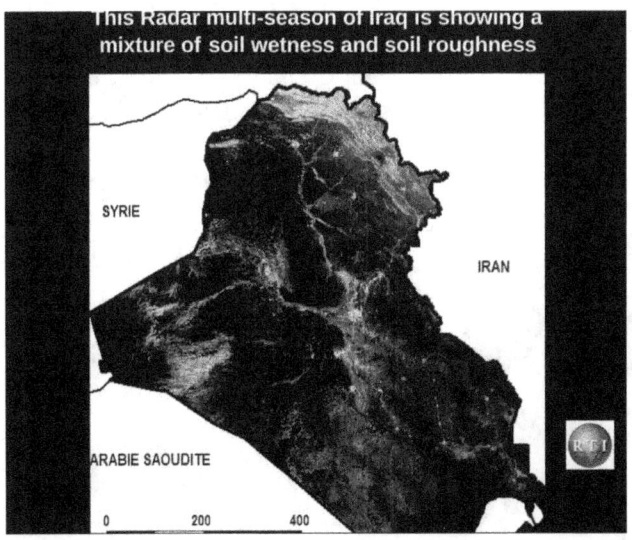

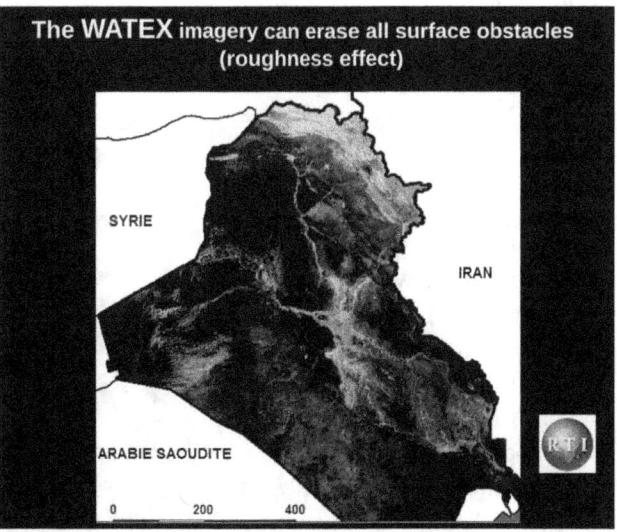

Agricultural potential is a key asset : today these abandoned wheat fields must be rehabilitated thanks to deep aquifers

Now, from this image, we have all the keys for the future reconstruction of Iraq. I speak only of Iraq, because I just studied Iraq; but you know, imagine the consequences for the rest of the region. Because this land, I come back here,—just focus here around Sinjar [Iraq], near Syria. **Slide 26** Huge plains, beautiful land, good soil. They can grow wheat, but the fields are abandoned because of the war, the silos empty; that has to be restored. We can put an end to the end of the world. This is the town of Sinjar; 300,000 persons live there. Completely destroyed!

New Vision of the World

For me, there are no desperate situations, without solutions. We must always remember that in life, you don't have problems, you have questions and answers. [Applause]

This new vision of the world reveals unknown groundwater resources. It leads decision-makers to prioritize their objectives, allows planning post-conflict reconstruction, quick and accurate action of great efficiency. The accuracy of these images is the size of the pixel, 6.5 meters. We know *exactly* where to go.

The new space technologies can change the groundwater geopolitical balance; but we should never forget that science must remain, above all, devoted to the service, *and* progress, of humanity.

Thank you very much. [Applause]

RAINER SANDAU

Towards a New Era of International Space Cooperation

Rainer Sandau is Technical Director, Satellites and Space Applications, of the International Academy of Astronautics.

Good afternoon. I want to thank Mme. Helga Zepp-La-Rouche for inviting me to give a talk about a topic which is close to my heart, but probably not that well known to you. And you will see there are some good connections to the overall theme of this conference, at the end.

This talk about the International Academy of Astronautics

(IAA) was prepared together with our Secretary General, Jean-Michel Contant; you will see him in some of the pictures. And first I want to talk about who we are, and what we do. And we *changed* to do better and more. The Academy was founded in 1960 by Theodore von Karman. He is probably known to you as one of the space pioneers leading the GALCIT project in Pasadena, now the Jet Propulsion Laboratory (JPL). And it is an international community of individuals, 1,200 active leading experts and 1,700 from 89 na-

April 12, 1961
Yuri Gagarin IAA Honorary Member
First Man in Space

16 June 1963
Valentina Tereshkova
IAA Honorary Member
On board Vostok 6
First Women Cosmonaut

March 1965
Alexei Leonov
IAA member
First Space Walk

tions; recognized by the UN in 1996, and the membership is based on strong competition, so it's not easy to join.

The aims of IAA are to—

• Foster the development of astronautics for peaceful purposes;

• Recognize individuals who have distinguished themselves in space science or technology;

• Provide a program through which members may contribute to international endeavors; and

• Promote international cooperation in the advancement of aerospace science.

I want to stress that it is an association of individuals. They can live their dreams and work on subjects which are not maybe in the interest of the entities they are coming from, in industry or organizations or so on; they are really free to work as individuals.

Leadership is through a high-ranking Board of Trustees, for instance 11 heads or former heads of space agencies are involved in that board. They do have six commissions covering all aspects of space activities, basic science, engineering science, life science, social sciences. And it offers the missing fora where the best experts in all domains can meet, know each other, and exchange their opinions. And that is really true, I can assure you.

Syria's Space Program

We do have regional secretariats in 30 regions, one of them in Syria. In Syria, we have a regional secretary, Dr. Hussein Ibrahim, who was a former general director of the General Organization of Remote Sensing.

And it's not well known, but Syria had a cosmonaut in space and had a good space program, but nowadays, of course, it's a problem. He is still a good friend of mine, but he hasn't been able to come to Germany in the last years because of visa problems. He obviously does not belong to the group of people which Madame Merkel invited to come to Germany, and he was always refused a visa.

Mme. Shaaban talked about these interesting sites, historical sites in Syria. And it crossed my mind that when I was first in Syria I was brought to that site, and I was excited about the history and the architecture. And I made a proposal at that time, 15 years ago, to use remote sensing techniques and information technology techniques, to make that site, the experience, available to people outside of Syria, in an adapted way and an interactive way.

So I have some good connections to Syria, as well.

IAA Firsts

Here is a glimpse of who is a member. I have selected some pictures which show the firsts: First man in space, Yuri Gagarin, is a member of our Academy. [**Slide 1**] By the way, that is the Secretary General of our Academy, Jean-Michel Contant, in the inset with Yelena Gagarina.

The first woman in space, Valentina Tereshkova. The first space walker, Alexei Leonov. [**Slide 2**] The first U.S. satellite, Explorer I, with IAA Academicians William Pickering, James van Allen, and Wernher von Braun. [**Slide 3**] They are all Academy members.

The first man on the Moon was Neil Armstrong.

First US satellite, Explorer 1: radiation belt theorized by James Van Allen, one of the outstanding discoveries of the International Geophysical Year.

Starting from left side: IAA Academicians William Pickering, James Van Allen, Wernher von Braun

Apollo 11, July 16-24, 1969, Neil Armstrong, IAA Member (left) commander,

Buzz Aldrin, IAA Member, (right) lunar module pilot.

Buzz Aldrin on July 20, 1969, completed a 2-hour and 15 minute lunar EVA

Here Buzz Aldrin, and it's close to 50 years ago! [**Slide 4**] Imagine that! Fifty years ago we went to the Moon, and it's an object of dreams.

The first world record we have in space is for the longest single spaceflight, one and a half years, held by Valeri Polyakov. [**Slide 5**]

And of course, connected with the Silk Road, Yang Liwei, the first Chinese astronaut, or taikonaut as they call it. [**Slide 6**]

We deal with studies and conferences: 18 to 20 IAA standalone conferences yearly. We have some glimpses here from Beijing, Bangalore, Moscow, and Fukuoka [**Slide 7**], in Berlin, as well—conferences. We do actually have 42 in preparation.

What you see here is what's already printed, dealing

World Record

The Soviet program was focusing on manned flight long duration experiment as exemplified by Mir crew member Valeri Polyakov, IAA member:
240 days in 1988 and unbroken record 437 days 17 hours and 58 minutes Soyuz TM-18 / Soyuz TM-20 January 8, 1994 to March 22, 1995

Successful Entry of China:
2003 Shenzhou V carrying China's first human in space
IAA Academician Yang Liwei

18 to 20 IAA Stand Alone Conferences Yearly

with different space-related subjects. [**Slide 8**] We have been a publishing house since 2012, with book series on small satellites—programs, missions, technologies, and applications; remote sensing of the Earth system, including science, technology, and applications; and proceedings of IAA conferences.

We have a space dictionary, free to be used. The last two contributions are in Gaelic and Afrikaans, always in connection with English, French, and German.

Cooperation with Emerging Countries

On our 50th anniversary, we decided to do something different, or something more, not just the academic activities, but to give the public a large moral output from our activities, so, we decided to build up a summit, a summit of the heads of space agencies, discussing possibilities for cooperation in four subjects: human space flight, planetary robotic exploration, climate change and green systems, and disaster management and natural hazards.

The background to these themes and initiatives is that many current cooperation projects are aging: ISS was initiated 20 years ago with only eight countries, and at that time more than half of today's space agencies did not exist.

Russia and the U.S.A. no longer taxi exclusively to space, and little cooperation with new space agencies in emerging countries has been established, by far not enough.

So the question now was, during that summit, how to balance new aspirations and challenge-solving, with existing programs, budgets, national interests, and needs? They are very different, from big countries to the emerging countries. How to cooperate with a large number of partners? How to build confidence, trust, transparency? How to share best practices? And how to ensure the safe and responsible use of space?

The Academy is a kind of catalyst. We are not the executive, but we can bring people together and try to have them work together. We are trying to work on concrete projects, studies, and pilot projects in the four areas I mentioned before, to prepare space cooperation for the new generations. You know, that's a cultural change. The situation we are facing right now is inherent in us, so we cannot jump over our shadows, but we have to prepare for the future.

So that was a historic summit with 30 heads of space agencies in Washington, in November 2010, in connec-

SLIDE 8

42 studies in preparation

IAA Studies
https://shop.iaaweb.org

SLIDE 9

Historic 30 Heads Space Agencies

tion with our 50th anniversary, and you see people sitting there, side by side and giving their agreement to the big idea of cooperation. [**Slide 9**]

Here you see a glimpse and the flavor of the spirit in that conference. The Vietnamese Pham Anh Tuan shaking hands with Charlie Bolden, the big guy; that wouldn't have happened before. [**Slide 10**] I hope it's an indication of what will happen in the future.

The goal of this summit was to reach a broad consensus on international cooperation at the highest level, and encourage new, concrete initiatives of cooperation in the four areas I mentioned before. And these four areas had already been prepared in IAA studies. You see here, for instance, the study is *Space-Application in Climate Change and Green Systems: The Need for International Cooperation*. And this is also true in the

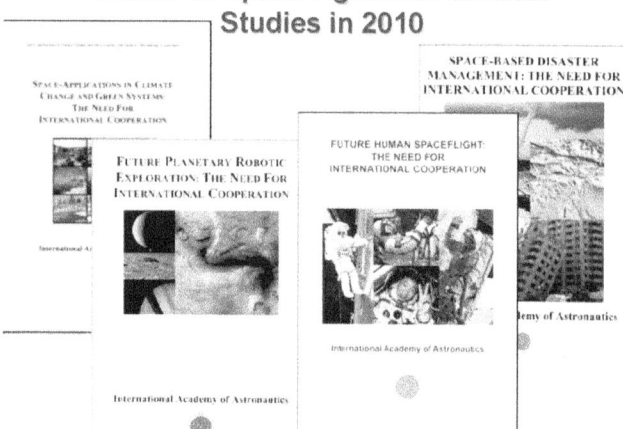

other three areas, for instance, *Future Planetary Robotic Exploration: The Need for International Cooperation*; *Future Human Spaceflight*; *Space-Based Disaster Management*. [**Slide 11**]

These are broad themes. They have to be broken down into tasks which can be acted on from both sides—the big guys, the smaller guys—and really task-relevant things have to be thought out in a form that you can work on it. So this prioritization was done in 2011, and we have a Steering Group and Coordination groups for the four different topics I mentioned.

We are now in the phase of concrete action. We are now discussing with 40-plus space agencies to make it happen.

There are a couple of follow-on conferences, meetings in 2012 for instance, in Kiev, Mysore, Naples. In Naples there were 14 heads of space agencies meeting and talking about specific topics.

And the recent milestones we've had were on more specific topics. We have four main topics, and these four main topics are for different kinds of agencies. That is, the developing countries are not that much involved right now in robotic missions and human space operations. But climate change and disaster management is a topic. So the first milestone was in January 2014, related to Planetary Robotic and Human Spaceflight Exploration, in Washington, again. And it was on that occasion that I had the opportunity and pleasure to meet Mme. Helga Zepp-LaRouche the first time, personally.

So that is a glimpse of the situation there. These are all heads of space agencies, meeting and working to-gether, at least, talking together. The working together is still a phase,— it's in the implementation, but it takes some time to make it really happen, and you know, everybody has his own budget, his own ideas, his own focus points, so they need to be aligned and synchronized; it takes time. But it's underway.

The second milestone for the two remaining topics, climate change and disaster management, took place in September in Mexico City, and this process is going on, discussing with more than 40 heads of space agencies, and breaking it down to the working level.

Together to Space, To Enrich All on Earth

So, to conclude: IAA is a unique elite body, to be a catalyst for cooperation on a new scale: "Together to Space, To Enrich All on Earth." And the intention is to persuade political decision makers to imagine space cooperation for the new generations' needs; to conclude and release new reports; and to make concrete proposals that the Summit follow-on can leverage.

I am convinced that this work fits pretty well into the theme of this conference. I hope I have been able to give you an insight into what's going on in this space area, which is for most people on Earth, a more exotic one. But it's not exotic, it's our daily life which is connected to space, and you don't even know what's going on and what you use from space. And I hope I have conveyed to you at least the idea of peaceful cooperation and have brought a positive perspective to this discussion after the mainly not so good results we have heard about in Syria and other countries right now.

EDITORIAL

The Time Has Come To Turn It Around

July 7—The following paraphrased exchange between Lyndon and Helga Zepp-LaRouche brought together many of the themes of a discussion between the two of them and the LaRouche PAC Policy Committee this morning.

Lyndon LaRouche: Between Helga and me, we've got to make some decisions, right now, about what we're going to do next, because we've got a lot of different directions we can go in. And the question is how Helga and I are going to act, in order to try to resolve the things we've got to settle right now.

Helga Zepp-LaRouche: The Brexit's implications are much, much bigger than we have noted.... You can see the fallout now in the financial sector: the six property hedge-funds which had to close down in London; the absolute desperation of the Bank of England. This thing is disintegrating. Then you will have the new election in Austria, which may very well bring in a government which will also lead Austria out of the EU, and that would be it. So we are in a period of absolute, on the one side, disintegration of the EU and the whole trans-Atlantic financial system.

Therefore, what I keep saying is that we have to get the whole organization singing from the same page on both sides of the Atlantic. We need to have this New Paradigm. And the New Paradigm has to be the joining with Russia and China in the "win-win" perspective, building a Silk Road extending into the United States, going for Glass-Steagall, going for a new credit system, and a new paradigm in terms of the identity of mankind. Because when I asked the man from the Naval War College, in light of the coincidence of all these crises coming at the same time,— doesn't it make sense to go to a higher level, and work together for the common aims of mankind? His answer was completely charac-

teristic for the kind of people who are the cause of the problem? He said, "I'm a pragmatic person, and I know about human nature, and this is the way it's always going to be: people will have conflicts." [Not an exact quote.] But that is the problem, because if mankind remains with that image of man, that human nature is such that man is incapable of rising to reason, then we will go under!

And therefore people really have to understand that the new paradigm, defining human civilization from a future standpoint of international collaboration in space travel, getting energy security through breakthroughs in fusion power, eliminating terrorism.

Terrorism is clearly out of control. Look at the number of terrorist events, from Istanbul to Indonesia, Bangladesh, and European countries. It's very clear that this is a showdown time, and the refusal to cooperate to work together against terrorism, and now with the Chechen trend being clearly in the Istanbul bombing,— who is controlling the Chechens? That goes way back to the old Chechen Wars.

So anybody who's not working together with Putin on the elimination of terrorism, is complicit in any future terrorist act which happens. And that's exactly what Senator Bob Graham had said: If the 28 pages had been published, even the Charlie Hebdo terrorist attack would not have happened. It's all one package, and people have to understand that this is now the unique moment, because the Chilcot Report is really not just an affair limited to Great Britain, because the whole [Iraq] war was based on lies, and the whole strategic picture really hangs together, and we must present it that way.

Lyndon: I would say,— just on the emergency level, because we're getting pressure on this question,— but I think the option of the Manhattan structure, the Manhattan system, is now ready to be used. It's not only ready to be used, it's got to be used, because only with an imperative being launched out of Manhattan or something like that, setting a rolling movement, and spreading it throughout the United States or as much as possible, can we probably break this thing. Because, is Obama going to bomb the world? Or is Obama going to give up? Or is he going to do something else in the middle? So the point is, I would say that the issue here, when you look at the facts, for sane people, the question would be: Shut this thing down! Shut this war down! Shut down the war and what it represents now!

The Real Question

You've got the thing from Britain, you've got things in Europe otherwise; you've got the things in other parts of the world. I think the time has come to push hard, and effectively, to shut this war down! Shut this kind of warfare—shut it down! Which means there's an obligation to create an economic system which will contribute to the needs of the population, both in the United States and elsewhere. Therefore, the question is not war. The question is, are the people of the United States prepared to reassemble themselves, and reconsider their destiny?

Are they willing to create a system of creation of wealth by people, and have that become the answer, the alternative to what's happening, for instance, in the United States, with all the people who are dying and suffering, as now? Therefore, are we going to find the alternative to that kind of nonsense, and similar kinds of nonsense? That's the question. Can we grab this thing, with the base probably around Manhattan? And I think we've got to really go hard on this thing, and get a real solid approach to say we are now really going to do the thing to save civilization, on the basis of what Manhattan has to offer.

We've got the United States. The United States has the ability to turn around. We've got enough to turn the clock around, to end this perpetual fear and evil. We've got to defend the United States in the sense of the people of the United States, by restoring the kind of system in the United States which is needed by the people, immediately, throughout the United States,— and encourage the people of other nations to accept the same option. I think it can be done; but it certainly *should* be done, regardless.

That's what we should be doing. I think it's our option. Grab it!

You're getting this "maybe" approach from the people [linked to the U.S. government] yesterday,— they are in doubt! And the question is, is Obama also ready to do the job that he wants to do? Or, are the people involved going to back down, and say, "Well, we're not going to go that far." And that's what we're looking for. Like what happened in Britain,— the British case. The government of Britain is now in a crisis of its existence. And similar kinds of situations are arising in other parts of the world. Isn't it possible that we can bring a concert of opinion among some people in some nations, to bring about the kind of agreement which solves this terrible problem?

The point is, we've come to a point in history where the condition of life of mankind, as mankind, can no longer accept the approach to something which is like Obama, and his predecessors. Therefore, the point is, why not struggle to create a movement which gives people a sense of saying, "Yes, you were right!" And doing it on time.

We can develop mankind. Einstein is a model person, to be considered in this connection. He didn't do everything, of course, but he did some things which were very important, and which most scientists have failed to consider.

People don't understand mankind. They get so fascinated with little things that they don't understand what mankind is. Mankind is unique. Mankind is the most beautiful thing known to us in the universe. So therefore, let's do it.

www.ingramcontent.com/pod-product-compliance
Lightning Source LLC
Chambersburg PA
CBHW080325290526
45793CB00006B/1211